Eating the Book

THE SEA HORSE IMPRINT

Paola Mieli, *Publisher & Director*
Mark Stafford, *Editor*
Richard G. Klein, *Research and Bibliography*
Martin Winn & Marie-Claude Hays, *Editorial Support*

This books is published under the aegis and with the financial assistance of Après-Coup Psychoanalytic Association, New York

Cover image: Detail of a ritual illustration of celebrants around a Seder table with the master of the house lifting the first cup, at the beginning of the Passover Haggadah, Illuminated ms., *The North French Miscellany*, 1277-1286, Additional 11639, f. 205, at the British Library.

Gérard Haddad

Eating the Book
Dietary Rites and Paternal Function

Translated by David Jacobson

Introduction by Luigi Ballerini

Agincourt Press
New York, 2013

Originally publised in French as *Manger le Livre: Rites alimentaires et fonction paternelle*, Éditions Grasset & Fasquelle, 1984; Éditions Hachette (Pluriel, Psychanalyse, with "Postface inédite," 2005).

Copyright © by Gérard Haddad 2013

ISBN: 978-1-946328-57-1

Design and typesetting
Danilo Montanari

Agincourt Press
P.O. Box 1039
Cooper Station
New York, NY 10003
www.agincourtpress.org

To Antonietta

"Ask ye now, and see whether a man doth travail with child? wherefore do I see every man with his hands on his loins, as a woman in travail, and all faces are turned into paleness?
Alas! for that day is great, so that none is like it..."

Jeremiah, XXX 6-7

Table of Contents

Luigi Ballerini, *Making sense: a few devout and unbridled observations on Gérard Haddad's* Eating the Book   p.   9

Framing the Problem   23

Part 1: The Father in Question   27
Chapter 1: From the Law of the Father to Fraternal Respect   29
Chapter 2: Thinking With One's Teeth   51

Part 2: The Discrete and the Continuous   61
Chapter 1: A Strange Meal   63
Chapter 2: From Writing to the Book   67
Chapter 3: The Birth of the Subject   83
Chapter 4: Writing and Fire   91
Chapter 5: The Raw, the Cooked … and the Symbolic   105
Chapter 6: The Book in the Freudian Field   127

Part 3: The Book and the Clinic   145
Chapter 1: Beyond a Clinic of Orality   147
Chapter 2: Proof from the Schizo   149
Chapter 3: The Dyslexic and His Father   155
Chapter 4: Medication and Psychosomatics   159
Chapter 5: The Alcoholic   161

Conclusion   173

Appendix: Signifying Transference   177

Acknowledgments   189

New Afterword: Table, Signifier, and Image   191

Luigi Ballerini
MAKING SENSE:
A FEW DEVOUT AND UNBRIDLED OBSERVATIONS ON GÉRARD HADDAD'S *EATING THE BOOK*

> Thought passes through a glass like a sunbeam,
> More swiftly still, for naught can hold it back.
> Petrarch, *Triumph of Eternity*, 34-35

"Good sense is, of all things in the world, the most equally distributed" writes, not without humor, René Descartes at the beginning of his *Discourse on the Method*. He then goes on to equate Good Sense and Reason, subsuming both under the function of "forming a good judgment and distinguishing the true from the false." Ultimately, and it's all in the first paragraph, he states that "the diversity of our opinions does not proceed from some men being more rational than others, but solely from the fact that our thoughts pass through diverse channels and the same objects are not considered by all. For to be possessed of good mental powers is not sufficient; the principal matter is to apply them well."

Delving into Gérard Haddad's *Eating the Book* in the wake of this Cartesian cautionary but nonetheless stimulating observation may prove surprisingly productive. First, however, we must familiarize ourselves with some of the implications inherent in the notion of good sense. While reason does not seem to need any particular prodding to be elected as a tool for understanding, good sense does not travel half as well. A whole slew of interrogatives spring up at the very mention of the term, and its kinship with common sense, which, though clearly postulated by Descartes, is in our own times often called into question.

Things stood quite differently not only in seventeenth century France, but all the way back to the first century of the so called Common Era, when Phaedrus, a learned Thracian slave who lived in Rome at the time of Augustus, and inscribed his name in the canon of Latin literature by versifying many of Aesop's prose fables in the langue of

Introduction

his masters, could equate brain power with good sense which, in fact, he called common:

> A fox, after looking by chance at a tragic actor's mask, remarked: "O what a majestic face is here, but it has no brains (*cerebrum non habet*). This is a twit for those to whom Lady Luck has granted rank and renown, but denied them common sense (*sensum communem*)."

It is worthy to notice, in passing, that, here, the notion of "good" is implanted in that of "common," rather than vice versa. Centuries later, past not only Phaedrus, but Descartes as well, in a radically different cultural environment, the commonality of good sense receded from its pole position: what is emphasized, indeed, is the rarity of its sightings, its tendency to hide in the depth of human conscience, whence individual talent alone has the power to extract it. In lines 41 to 46 of the "Epistle to Richard Boyle, Earl of Burlington," contained in his *Moral Essays* (also known as *Epistles to Several Persons*) Alexander Pope extols the praises of good sense as follows:

> Some there is more needful than Expence
> And something previous, ev'n to taste—t 'is Sense:
> Good Sense, which is the only gift of Heaven,
> and though no science, fairly worth the seven,
> a light, which in yourself you must perceive;
> Jones and Le Nôtre have it not to give.[1]

Whatever sense—good or common, or both—might have meant for Lewis Carroll, he certainly subjects it to a sensationally amusing *tour de force* in Chapter IX (as well as elsewhere) of his *Alice*

---

[1] For a better understanding of the quotation, readers should be advised that by "the seven," Pope means the seven sciences of the medieval curriculum: the *trivium* (grammar, logic, and rhetoric), plus the *quadrivium* (music, arithmetic, geometry, and astronomy). The celebrated Inigo Jones (1573-1651), known as the "English Palladio," was the official architect to Queen Anne and presided over the restoration of St. Paul's Cathedral (1633). André Le Nôtre (1613-1700) was, in Pope's own view, "the designer of the best gardens in France" among which: Versailles and Fontainebleau, both of them expression of the then prevailing "esprit de géométrie."

in Wonderland where he relates "The Mock Turtles Story." Here's a scrap from the exchange between Alice and the Duchess:

> "'Tis so," said the Duchess: "and the moral of that is – 'Oh, 'tis love, 'tis love, that makes the world go round!'"
> "Somebody said," Alice whispered, "that it's done by everybody minding their own business!"
> "Ah, well! It means much the same thing," said the Duchess, digging her sharp little chin into Alice's shoulder as she added, "and the moral of *that* is—'Take care of the sense, and the sounds will take care of themselves.'"
> "How fond she is of finding morals in things!" Alice thought to herself.

Above and beyond the whimsical equation of "love" and "minding one's own business," proposed by the Duchess—a logician *sans pareil*—, the passage features two semantic occurrences of great importance: one is the willful spin Alice puts on the term "moral" that, uttered first as a synonym of *conclusion, consequence, sum, essence, juice* etc., migrates, ironically to be sure, to the domain of ethical concerns. The other is the idea that sense is something one has to take care of, i.e., something one has to make: "Take care of the sense and the sounds will take care of themselves", urges the Duchess.

The latter concern obtains as well, and prominently, in the quest undertaken by Gérard Haddad in the pages of his *Eating the book*, where the two terms of the binomial are, however, surprisingly reversed: "Take care of the sound and the sense will take care of itself."

At the risk of spoiling, through premature exposure, much of the pleasure that can be drawn from a savoring of the linguistic, analytical, and exegetical ingredients that make up Haddad's work, I shall bring up, at this juncture, an illuminating example of this glorious reversal. First, however, we must caution that in our day and age, the isometric oscillation of the sensible pendulum between good and common are nowhere to be found (and measured), due to the deplorable conditions under which the latter term is forced to operate: the sharing of good sense is not impeded by the diversity of channels through which it is made to circulate, as Descartes had suggested, but rather by the colonization of its premises carried out by standardized means of information. Whatever it is that we call communication, there is hardly anything left in it of what it originally signified: the acquisition of wis-

Introduction

dom made possible through a communal effort. What we have instead is the imposition of a pre-fabricated knowledge, a-critically imposed on an ever increasing number of subjects rendered incapable of any reaction whatsoever. The assembly, the *ecclesía*, is gone, or merely preserved as an empty shell.²

And now the example: in it the author pulverizes a traditional and commonly held view and, by carefully parsing the molecular structure of an essential signifier, enables a slice of the scriptural text to resonate in manners that, while at first seemingly preposterous, are quickly recognized as plausible, indeed as necessary, to the unveiling of the symbolical value underlying the narrative. An endlessly repeated explanation has accreted into a receptacle of common sense which, as the result of Haddad's analysis, will prove to be anything but good.

The story goes that because of their hasty departure from Egypt, the Hebrews did not have time to let their bread rise. Though the letters of both *Exodus* and *Deuteronomy* explicitly state this as a fact, and imposes, on occasion, the eating of *matzoh* ("the bread of affliction") as a reminder of the event that put an end to their long enslavement, the commandments given to Moses date several days before the great event of the liberation. "The notion of haste," Haddad points out,

> is not included, the Hebrews having been told well in advance that they would have to eat unleavened bread. The explanations tradition gives for this prescription will bear curiously not upon the unleavened bread—*matzoh*—but on its opposite, the *hamatz*, a term that designates the leaven or yeast, but also all fermentation, all mold. If prevalence, in regard to a rite, is given to the signifier, isn't it remarkable that *matzoh/hamatz* forms an opposed pair of terms in anagram, a new illustration of the insistence of the laws of language that the rite inculcates in the subject with an explicit violence?

The textual anomaly or, more precisely, the inadequacy of the traditional explanation, is seized upon by the author of *Eating the Book* as an opportunity to search for that which exceeds the accepted and

---

² The extreme circumstances under which we labor are probably typical of our mediatic age and did not exist prior to it, but attempts at dumbing down knowledge to levels of homogenized and autocratic information have been carried in the past as well, through preaching, formulaic teaching, etc.

ultimately tranquillizing elucidation. A rationalization that had been benignly digested and passed on from one generation to the next (the followers of Moses were, no doubt, in a great hurry to leave Egypt), is probed and fathomed to cause what has been overlooked in it (the "objective correlatives" of leaven, such as swelling, and in turn, pride, narcissism, and similar bad principles, that must be "hunted down") to release an unexpected and by far more rewarding cognitive result.

In a manner that is reminiscent of what, in his essay on historical semantics, the great philologist Leo Spitzer identifies as a swerve, a deviation from the stylistic norm of a writer, Haddad elects what is hermeneutically unconvincing as his point of departure for a journey fueled, essentially, by etymology and mental associations. A "commonsensical" explanation, that could be accepted only if no further questions were to be asked, is thus re-opened and given a new chance to make good sense, that is: to grow and fructify in the mind of readers spurred by an unquenchable curiosity. Haddad writes:

> Consulting a dictionary ... we discover that *matzoh* signifies "to press," "squeeze," as, for instance, juice from a fruit. But also that it is a form of the verb *matsats*, "to suck." Thus the unleavened bread would condense two fundamental terms: the dripping or flowing out, as of some overripe fruit, of the people of Israel from its Egyptian containment, as well as the relation to the breast, sucking.
>
> At this point it is necessary to re-read the whole of this epic that was the flight out of Egypt. A narrow receptacle[3] in which the descendants of a single man, Jacob, will multiply so much that their presence will prove awkward yet their departure also seem difficult. The body of Egypt subjected to those terrible convulsions that are the plagues, repetitive, prolonged, until the moment of possible expulsion of Israel ... The great battered body of Egypt expels, in trauma, a little body, a new nation, radically different from it.
>
> If this epic has such a deep hold upon the reader, even the non-Jewish one, it is because it represents, with an exceptional vividness, a prodigious staging in which the birth of a people reflects that of every little person. Is it any wonder that at this point the first food, this *matzoh-sucking*, should contain an echo of the breast?

---

[3] The inhabitable area of Ancient Egypt did not extend much beyond the banks of the Nile: hence the notion of a long and narrow country.

It is not the purpose of these introductory notes to follow in details the splendid flights of signifiers that lead the author, and the excited reader he has in tow, from breast to birth, to separation, to the imposition of the law, to the paternal function, and beyond this, to the various pathologies that an improper handling of their cultural and psychic projections may cause: fields through which the author meanders with consummate skill and competence.

It is necessary, however, to point out that one of the main axes, if not the principal axis, around which *Eating the Book* revolves, is a reframing of the perspective within which to assess the Freudian notion of the primitive father, cannibalistically devoured by his children. As it is well known, this notion constitutes a corner stone of the entire Freudian edifice and its destiny has often been associated with that of totemic theories that have, progressively, fallen short of the mark. Wittingly reminding his readers that Freud is in the right even when he makes "mistakes," the author shows how a thoroughly dynamic and radically new appraisal of the entire conundrum can be performed by following a surprising and hitherto un-trodden path.

Hearkening back to the book that concern us here, in the early pages of a later publication (*Les Folies millénaristes*, 2001), Haddad very aptly synthesizes the profile of his quest:

> [In my *Eating the book*] I investigated a number of nutritional rites such as they are actually performed, beginning with those with which I am most familiar: the nutritional rites of the Jews, varied and complex as they can be. Unexpected and yet unavoidable conclusions could be reached by means of this investigation: Freud's symbolic Father, "cannibalistically" devoured in the primary identification, materializes in the Book ... whose incorporation empowers the subject to acquire the imprescriptible sentiment of belonging to a human family, to a people.

The subtraction of meaning from the sphere of the immediately referential, and the activation of a subject capable of transcending habits of reason sanctioned by the assumed necessity of proving the validity of their premises, introduce a new way of making good sense which we could only hope to see adopted far and wide, within and without the boundary of the psychoanalytical cure.

The discovery that food-related signifiers are indeed carriers of hidden historical truths leads to the equation of *reading* and *eating*, and clearly supports the establishment of a transparent link between the reality of the symbolic Father stipulated by Freud and its actual manifestation in the form of the written document.

This implies a thoroughly philological probing of pertinent scriptural passages, down to their lexical, grammatical, and even phonological components (much in the vein of Lacan's *Insistence of the Letter in the Unconscious*), and the adoption of a reading method predicated on the notion of the *signifying transference*, a concept and a technique that runs through the entire book. Conscious of the difficulty inherent in a full appreciation of what the process of the *signifying transference* might entail, Haddad has chosen to conclude his book with an appendix, in which the text of a 1981 lecture is reproduced.[4] Here the notion is brought to the fore in terms that could not be clearer, and readers should perhaps refer to it as soon as they encounter the term. Having alerted us that the traditional "conceptual" method of reading Freud

> involves dangers: those resulting from the privilege accorded to signification, to imagination, indeed to the "idolizing" of concepts. It tends, to a greater or lesser extent, to reabsorb the heterogeneity of the Freudian text, to return the singularity of analytic discourse to preexisting, essentially philosophical, universals

Haddad proposes an undaunted return to an investigative

> approach that would aim less at digging for discoveries than questioning the very train, the progress, of the thought, the connections, the involuntary associations that the various texts themselves make [...] Rather than visit the countries arrived at, we would be interested in the voyage itself, in the paths that Freud managed to take in order to say what he said. [...] The method, heavy as it may seem, is immediately fertile and at once provides certain valuable results. It allows us to recall, first of all, that the different Freudian concepts can only with difficulty be isolated from one another, that they indubitably form a Borromean chain.

---

[4] First read at the Martin-Buber Institut of the University of Brussels, November 1981.

Introduction

Not only this: having introduced a principle of fragmented but joinable continuity in a world ruled, symptomatically, by sameness and opposition, the author pulls from his psychoanalytical top hat the rabbit of analogy, a term much praised by many exponents of early twentieth century European avant-garde movements, chief among them F. T. Marinetti ("Analogy is but the deep love that connects distant objects") and André Breton ("It is erroneous to claim that the mind has grasped the relationship of two realities in the presence of each other. First of all, it has seized nothing consciously. It is, as it were, from the fortuitous juxtaposition of the two terms that a particular light has sprung, *the light of the image*, to which we are infinitely sensitive."). Analogy then is making sense out of what, at first sight, seems anything but analogous.

To bring the point home, Haddad reminds us that "the finest illustration of this procedure" in which, clearly, the essential part of the engine is provided by the method of free association,

> is probably to be found in the article 'The Theme of the Three Caskets.' Freud uses two plays by Shakespeare, a comedy, *The Merchant of Venice*, and a tragedy, *King Lear*. The former contains the episode of the *three* caskets, the latter that of King Lear's *three* daughters. The occurrence of the term *three* is enough for Freud to identify their significations.

The power of persuasion of a signifying transference, Haddad reminds us, is often enhanced by the presence of verifiable etymological links: as is the case, both exquisite and galvanizing, with which Freud chose to illustrate the notion of transference itself.

> "Transference," he [Freud] writes, "may be compared to the intermediary layer between the tree and the bark, a layer that provides the starting-point for the formation of new tissues and the augmentation of the trunk's thickness."

This same metaphor, "between tree and trunk," is likewise found elsewhere to designate the unconscious itself, in Freud as in Lacan.

Now, as it happens, in botany, this "between bark and tree" is called *liber*, the etymology precisely for the Latin *liber*, "book," [...] since the first medium for writing was this intermediary layer easily detachable in certain species.

Implicitly, then, Freud offers us a theory of the transference structured like a book.

All this, necessarily, calls for a careful re-definition of the role of reader, of the person or the community committed to making sense of a text, any text, really, but of course the issue must be dealt with greater courage, and a much deeper sense of responsibility, when the text is such that a whole society (no matter how diversified) finds, in the rites described therein, the reasons of its cohesiveness, its *raison d'être*. Before such sacred texts (of which *The Quran* and *The Bible* are supreme examples, of course) an "indifferent" or "non-amorous" reading, one in which the reader invests "a faint curiosity that could either burgeon or end abruptly, in quest of information, or relaxation," is hardly conceivable:

> In total opposition to this is a second, "loving" form of reading—with its underside of hatred—that we prefer to call *canonic*. A certain number of books, among them the "sacred" texts, are the object of another sort of treatment. They are not suited to relaxation but rather to study, often requiring painful effort. One never tackles them without certain wariness, indeed without rituals, in a relation strongly tinged with anxiety. In the face of so many difficulties, the common run of mortals give up not on owning them but on reading them.

It is like saying that indifferent readers do not make any sense, in the *sense* that they do not contribute to its making, and merely accept some pre-established configuration of it, getting excited, at best, at the various devices deployed by an author to delay a conclusion that has been known all along. Canonic or loving readers, on the other hand, are faced with at least three options: some may presume that a definitive truth can be extracted from a text written in stone, as it were, rather than on paper or parchment, and that it must be taken in as formulated by those who are in the know and claim, furthermore, to own a reading patent issued by God himself. Others have given up on the notion of divine authority only and claim that everyone has equal access to the truth expressed in the text (even when the sense is hard to crack). Others still practice a type of guided reading: guided, that is, as far as the method is concerned, but not iron-clad in some hermeneutical fixation.

While the first two options, or categories, as it might be preferable to call them, are somewhat padlocked in a short addendum that has appeared only in the latest edition of *Eating the Book* (and is duly

Introduction

reproduced here), the third *modus legendi*—which, let us not forget, implies that reading is first and foremost an act of *tying together*—pervades Haddad's book from top to bottom: its name is *Midrash*, the Jewish way of reading the Bible.

Entering, at this juncture, a concise list of the advantages and the surprises inherent in this luxuriating textual approach, would result in a display of uncalled for clumsiness. Thus, I will merely grant myself the privilege of confessing the sincere enthusiasm and actual devotion I feel for a type of interpretation that, no matter how far and wide its net is cast, is always a) rooted in the materiality of the letter in which it is inscribed, b) eager to engage the dialogical proximity with texts that can be made to interact with the sample of writing under scrutiny, and c) openly conscious of the tradition created by the opinions of earlier interpreters.

Curiously these opinions are not regarded, pragmatically, as some sort of authoritative verdicts, but rather as opportunities to destabilize convictions, in an incessant relaying of thoughts that will never crystallize into an unshakeable pyramid of beliefs. From the point of view of the Midrashic reader, the text is "a hub of interrelation, a crossroad waiting to acquire sense."[5]

Given that sense to be extracted from a composition of words can only be obtained by resorting to another composition of words, a rather strong Midrashic quality must be recognized in Derrida's notion of *différance* whereby meaning is an experience burgeoning out of movement, which necessarily creates interstices, and deferral, which creates an endless waiting-for, a perennial tending-to. Would it be too much to say that even the words used by Paul of Tarsus to assuage the fears and hesitations of his "brothers and sisters," and confirm the second coming of the Lord (and with it the end of time), belie a Midrashic vein?

> Now concerning the time and the season [...] you do not need to have anything written to you. For you yourself know very well that the day of the Lord will come like a thief in the night. When they say, "There is peace and security," then sudden destruction will come upon them, as labor pains come upon a pregnant woman, and there will be no escape!

---

[5] Expression borrowed from David Banon, *Le Midrach* (Paris, Press Universitaires de France, 1995).

But you, beloved, are not in darkness, for that day to surprise you like a thief; for you are all children of light and children of the day; we are not of the night or of darkness. So let us not fall asleep as others do, but let us keep awake and be sober; for those who sleep sleep at night, and those who are drunk get drunk at night. But since we belong to the day, let us be sober and put on the breastplate of faith and love, and for a helmet, the hope of salvation.[6]

Here the time in between, the time of non-fulfillment, ceases to configure as a time of anxiety. Waiting no longer means time spent vegetating in the obsession that prevents thought from becoming action. It means, on the contrary, constructing in broad daylight the cognitive morphology of one's own awareness. The notions that in ordinary linguistic exchange are associated with waiting (length, duration, sequential development, etc.) are replaced by the likes of tension, tending, in-tending, alertness, and the experience of a heightened sensibility.[7] Unlike an apple ripened by the passing of the seasons, the ripening of the human being is generated internally, by the guided (and not fettering) acquisition of the art of thinking.

The loving, canonic reading, of which the *midrash* constitutes a supreme example, can perhaps lead us out of the century old conflict between believing and thinking, and ultimately reach behind the sarcasm (which is not the same as suppressing it) that lies at the core of a most celebrated verse by Charles Baudelaire. Drawing our attention to a *Hypocrite lecteur*, the poet unmasks him as his "semblable" and his "frère." We too, adhering to the movement of the signifying transference, and extracting from the signifier *hypocrite* (commonly held to apply to a dissembler of ideals, to a person who plays a part he does not subscribes to) its full etymological pregnancy may cleanse it of all moralistic encrustations, and return it to the purity of its original function: that of an actor, the performer of a task, an individual who, far from being viewed as reprehensible, gets promoted to a higher level of responsibility in the activity of making sense out of a text.

In *Eating the Book* sense is brilliantly made, as previously mentioned, by probing Jewish rituals that when mechanically observed

---

[6] *First Letter to the Thessalonians*, 5, 1-8.
[7] "An immense, long, deliberate *derangement* of all the senses" Rimbaud might have added. See his *Lettre du Voyant*.

Introduction

might seem peculiar and even downright absurd, but when deeply and fully appreciated in their linguistic structure acquire a revelational status. Having remarked that, in Judaism, hardly a food related event can occur lest it is accompanied by utterances and inscribed in the performance of a rite, no matter how slight and seemingly negligible its features, Haddad writes:

> It's no mystery, then: the main effect expected of the *kashrut* is *psychological*; it forms the basis for the feeling of community in a mechanism of identification. An author as eminent as Maimonides sought to propose other reasons, hygienic and medical, for these dietary laws, but tradition has rejected them, by reckoning that the moral and psychological aspect outweighs every other consideration.

Wry as his comments and musings may, on occasion, be—when, for instance, he feigns stupor before the possibility that the morsel of pumpkin swallowed at a *Seder* may have a symbolic value, or when he characterizes as a "symbolic sandwich" the fact that no pious Jew would ever eat, even the smallest particle of food without pronouncing a ritual formula before and after the ingestion—Haddad never loses sight of the primary goal of his quest which is that of showing how the Jewish way of making sense, as embedded in the dietary rites enunciated in the *Torah* and elaborated in the Rabbinic Literature, are a formidable and indeed privileged angle from which to assess the *forma mentis* that made possible the "invention" of psychoanalysis.

The proof may indeed be in the *Charosheth* (a fruit pudding eaten at Passover meals that functions as a memory aid for the clay with which the Israelites made bricks during their Egyptian captivity). Decoding of the symbolic value of an actual ingestion as the conveyance of a sensible language-based message—a fact of which there remain thin but indelible traces in everyday parlance: can't a book be "devoured," and how many texts have found, in our own experience, not so easily "digestible"?—is vividly supported by a number of scriptural, Talmudic and Kabalistic examples, such as the great vision of the prophet Ezekiel:

> And when I looked, behold, a hand was sent unto me; and, lo, a roll of a book *was* therein; And he spread it before me; and it *was* written within

and without: and *there was* written therein lamentations, and mourning, and woe. Moreover he said unto me, Son of man, eat that thou findest: eat this roll, and go speak unto the house of Israel.[8]

or that of its Christian remake, by John, in the *Book of Revelation*:

And I saw another mighty angel come down from heaven .... And he had in his hand a little book open .... And the voice which I heard from heaven spoke unto me again, and said, go *and* take the little book which is open in the hand of the angel which standeth upon the sea and upon the earth. / And I went unto the angel, and said unto him, Give me the little book. And he said unto me, Take *it*, and eat it up: and it shall make thy body bitter, but it shall be in thy mouth sweet as honey. / And I took the little book out of the angel's hand, and ate it up; and it was in my mouth sweet as honey: and as soon as I had eaten it, my belly was bitter./ And he said unto me, Thou must prophesy again before many peoples, and nations, and tongues, and kings.[9]

The ethnological conclusions upon which early examples of analytical curiosity were based or used to buttress their arguments, some formulated by Freud himself, have not held up to a more sophisticated ethnological scrutiny, or to the discovery of new data. Yet, Haddad points out, the pertinence of Freud's observations remains intact: viewed through the glasses of the signifying transference, the examined phenomena activate a relentless search for meanings that have a direct bearing on daily life and never cease to produce truths that are both cogent and renewable.

Eating the Book felicitously shows how sense—good, helpful, unsuspected sense—unearthed from the sphere of religion and, more precisely, from some structural elements of a particular liturgy, can migrate to that of a discourse endowed with a very specific therapeutic function. Actually, somewhere between the lines of the book, there seems to stir a greater ambition: the inauguration of a liberating grammar, the acquisition of new lexical acceptations, and a paratactic way of connecting thoughts, expressing emotions, and signifying the individual's relationship to his tribe. I recommend Haddad's stunning

---

[8] Ezekiel, 2, 9-10; 3, 1.
[9] John, 10.

Introduction

contribution to the care and attention of those readers who believe that sense can be returned to its pristine status of being both good, common, and actively enhanced by all. A titanic enterprise, to be sure.

New York, June 2013

FRAMING THE PROBLEM

The Oedipus complex is a mith dreamed by Freud, a dream that has remained undeciphered. Lacan saw the matter, at the end of his work, at the farthest reaches of his critique of Freudian theories.[1] Freud preferred this mythical form to a direct approach to the question of the father, thus evading the terrible ordeal of confronting El-Shaddai, the religion of his fathers, an intellectual framework to which, for all his non-belief, he was tied by every fiber of his soul.

This is the point, roughly where Lacan ended, from which I had to start out again, first making certain that psychoanalysis and Midrash are in fact isomorphic. Verifying this exceeded all my expectations, and taking that step backward has allowed me to state in Leninesque fashion: psychoanalysis is Midrash plus castration. In a previous book[2] I examined to what extent psychoanalytical *technique*—the art of reading within the discourse of the patient—was, oddly enough, none other than a massive return of ancient Jewish Midrash, a return denied, misunderstood even, by "enlightened" Jews, and returning in the wake of the Viennese physician, to plough up and shake to its depths all modern thought about man.

This solid anchoring point is thus the starting place for deciphering the Freudian dream.

What path do we take? As ever, the one that defines man as a speaking being. And indeed, as far as we explore it, every human fact always reveals a weaving together of language, an established principle ever since Freud's first, inspired women patients revealed to him the structure, in "stupid wordplay," of the neurotic symptom, and

---

[1] Jacques Lacan, *Le Séminaire livre XVII, l'Envers de la psychanalyse*, 1969-1970 (Paris: Éditions du Seuil, 1991) (The Seminar: Book XVII, *The Other Side of Psychoanalysis*, NY, W.W. Norton, trans. Russell Grigg.)

[2] Gérard Haddad, *L'enfant illégitime, sources talmudiques de la psychanalyse*, 1981, 2nd edition 1990, 3rd edition, Desclée de Brower, 1996.

ever since structural thought, rushing into the breach, broadened the scope of this revelation.

This hold language has over man is so deep-set, so primordial, that a question immediately arises: How does language come to man, by what strange mechanism does it slip so tightly into the Nessus' shirt of structure?

Is biological determinism at work here? This factor is not to be denied, yet very clearly it proves insufficient. The case of Victor "the wild child of Aveyron"[3] established that over a century ago. We don't acquire language innately but rather through an "otherness" that grasps onto us from the first moment we enter life. Language comes to a given subject through the group into which he is born, through a particular language commonly referred to as a mother tongue. The subject is taken hold of there, where he is joined to a cultural group, and through his particular language is integrated into the world and its categories of thought, in a definitive knot which death alone will untie.

Hence our question—how does language reach man?—turns out to involve another burning question, that of the relation of the individual to the group. It projects onto the horizon the enigma linguistics refuses to take up, that of the origin of language itself. Through its different connections, does it not provide an Ariadne's thread for a new reading of Freud, from his first writings on aphasia to his last, on Moses?

We expect this question to shed new light by which to redefine the paternal function, that enigma that informs Judaism more than any other culture.

* * *

Freud was wont to recall, throughout his writings, from the first to the last,[4] that human beings are diphasic. Man's sexuality, for ex-

---

[3] Jean Itard, *Mémoire et rapport sur Victor de l'Aveyron*, in: Lucien Malson, *Les enfants sauvages*, 1964, Union générale d'édition, collection dirigée par Christian Bourgois.

[4] Sigmund Freud, *An Outline of Psychoanalysis*, in *S.E.*, vol. XXIII. (All quotations of Freud's works will henceforth refer to the *Complete Works* in the English edition, the *Standard Edition* (London: Hogarth Press, 1974, 1975, 1978).

ample, was acquired only in a process divided into two quite far-flung times: earliest childhood and adulthood.

This remark holds true also for his own oeuvre, which is marked by a deep inflection, a dialectical moment in his development, not a rupture, that can be dated to 1906, a year that witnessed so many other scientific and political upheavals.

There is a first period, then: 1895-1905. In this decade, Freud discovers the Unconscious, that otherness of language dividing every subject into two scenes; one, consciousness, whose innermost recesses the philosophers had explored, and another, radically separate. He explores the principal mechanisms of this "Other scene," clearing the main access routes to it, providing for those who wish to follow it a perfectly coded instruction manual: free association, couch, armchair, with a technique of interpretation to boot. The accent falls, then, on the singularity of the subject, isolated, or nearly so, from the social fabric, reduced to private life, to the family circle, with this unheard-of discovery: prohibition of incest is the mechanism for every individual drama.

Anyone but Freud would have remained content to be the caretaker of that enormous discovery, at most polishing away its imperfections, since such advances usually drain the mind and spirit they've been born into. In the wake of this first period marked by the deciphering of hysteria, psychoanalysis might have remained a discipline dedicated to the individual in his private life.

But from 1906 on, Freud felt he was being summoned elsewhere. Even before, in his first paces, between 1893 and 1895, he devoted himself, with some urgency, to an apparently secondary operation: amid the bric-à-brac of psychiatry as practiced then, he attempted to establish a surer classification of the field of the neuroses by defining a new nosographical class, the *Zwangsneurose*, or obsessional neurosis, up to then an impenetrably murky area in which "doubting mania (*folie de délire*)," "monomania," and "delirium of touch" covered both serious psychotic ailments and neurotic manifestations. This new entity Freud carved out would become his privileged object of study at the same time that his interest in hysteria was waning.

The study of this obsessional neurosis, which he would occasionally call antisocial neurosis, would persuade Freud to identify the connection that links the subject to the group as the very means by which language is acquired. An unassuming article, "Obsessive Acts and Religious Practices,"⁵ provides the first landmark in this shift, by creating an analogy between religious ritual and obsession that would become as famous as it is misunderstood. It reads like a preface to the important revisions that Freud would make to his doctrine.

This notion of two stages in Freudian theory is well known. Analyst authors are in the habit of calling these stages the first and second topics. I want, however, to introduce a new element, developing my thesis of a masked dialogue between Freud and his religion as the misrecognized basis of his oeuvre, by positing that each of these two topics corresponds to the two great aspects of Jewish culture: *Haggada* (or Midrash) and *Halacha*.

The first period of Freud's thought bears witness to the secret wedding of Freud and Midrash, the triumphant re-finding of the letter, the fantasy of anagrams and of flashes of wit, the small narratives that light up the whole.⁶ This first period is undoubtedly marked by a sort of felicity of writing, the enthusiasm of the discoverer, but also by a great solitude.

In the present work I hope to show that the second topic covers, in part, this inevitable but profoundly failed rendezvous between Freud and *Halacha*—the dominant branch of Jewish literature which established once and for all religious ritual and social legislation, regulating the relations of the individual to his peers and thus to the group.

Stated so bluntly, this thesis may well sound startling. The arguments that underpin it will be steadily laid out. The operation promises, beyond any theoretical gain, to be of both clinical and (no need to blush!) therapeutic interest.

---

⁵ S. Freud, "Obssessive Acts and Religious Practices," *S.E.* vol. IX.
⁶ This aspect therefore was the object of my book *L'Enfant illégitime* [cf. note 3].

PART ONE

THE FREUDIAN FATHER IN QUESTION

Chapter 1

FROM THE LAW OF THE FATHER TO FRATERNAL RESPECT

The obsessional is a man or woman for whom certain acts in life seem mysteriously interfered with by some added-on activity, stupid and utterly senseless even for the person directly affected by it.

For ten years after first noting this, Freud produces few writings on this question, until his 1906 article on rituals. But from then on, he devotes to it the better part of his energy, placing it immediately after his well-known texts on "anal erotism," on "the Rat Man," and, crowning this group, the book *Totem and Taboo*. The offensive is waged now on all fronts. The inaugural place of the text on rituals thus justifies our pausing to consider it.

A second event is clearly marked in these pages. For the first time, Freud is putting into writing, publicly broaching, a question close to his heart: religion, up to this point bashfully covered up by the term *Oedipus complex*.

And for barely a few months now Freud has his first distinguished student, Carl Jung, in his midst—he too is fascinated by religious questions. Jung has made his way to Vienna for a first encounter with the master, who invites him to the Wednesday meetings and, at one of these, himself delivers, in the visitor's presence, an exposé of the very article I have been referring to. It is his way of showing this student—whose mystical tendencies have been noted—the good way to proceed in this field. And what way is that?

Freud had gained important knowledge about obsession but not yet shared it publicly. He had deciphered its stupid rites and ascertained that every element in them referred to some unconscious signification, and some language structure. The woman, for instance, who had to sit on one particular chair, was declaring her wish to have lovers to console her for her unhappy marriage. At the same time the obsessional rites reveal an "unconscious consciousness of guilt": at every moment the obsessed person awaits some terrible punishment for temptations of a sexual nature. His ritual is already the start of an expiation, or rather a compromise between temptation and expiation. As it turns out, this knowledge, briefly recalled, hangs entirely on one term: *ceremonial*.

The "good way" that Freud points to consists in noting that this same term is essential in another domain as well, whose autonomy he himself underlines in relation to psychopathology, namely, religion. This double occurrence of a single term leads him to attempt a strange operation, which should surprise and shock only our most set ways of thinking: to transfer, by dint of this same word, his knowledge of the field of psychopathology to that of religion. All the epistemology in the world will not be able to find the philosophical reason behind this operation. A superficial examination would suggest that it amounts to an analogy. Yet if that's what it is, it's of a different sort than Aristotle's "*a* is to *b* as *c* is to *d*."

Once this operation is pointed out, before long we find it over and over again, in the earlier text on screen memories, and later at each critical juncture in Freud's oeuvre. Soon it appears to be *the very motor* of the developments, the steady broadening out, of all of Freud's thinking.[7]

As it happens, this same operation exists as such in the Midrash and the Talmud, perhaps as the preeminent rule for interpretation: the *gezera chava*, or "same rules," for which I have proposed the term of *signifying transference* in order to denote its general use in the Talmud, psychoanalysis, and anthropology.

It may well constitute Freud's most massive borrowing from Midrash, generally extending the rule of contiguity of statements, or *semikha*.

The interest of the signifying transference made between obsession and religion does not consist, as analogy would have it, in pointing out their phenomenological resemblances—the same remorse when the ceremonial is omitted, the same meticulousness in performing it—but rather in penetrating their signification. It allows us these two decisive propositions: because obsessive ritual possesses unconscious significations—as does religious ritual, as well—and because obsession

---

[7] More on this topic in Appendix. See p. 161.

stems from the repression of a drive, religion corresponds to an analogous mechanism, to an attempt at compromise between a guilty wish and a repressive interdiction.

Should we therefore, as some people would, identify the two structures? Obviously not. How are we, then, to class together the large social, public, collective manifestations of religious ceremonial with the solitary, secret, asocial ritual of the obsessive?

At this point Freud takes an important step, one that heralds the essence of his work to come: the repressed drive is of a different nature in these two cases. The neurotic represses a *sexual drive*, being unresigned in his unconscious to the prohibition of incest; religion, for its part, represses a selfish *ego drive*, placing a ban on antisocial, murderous tendencies by pronouncing: "Thou shalt not kill." In a few words, Freud grasps—rediscovering the style of the great Hillel—the core of the religious phenomenon, the imperative "Thou shalt love thy neighbor as thyself," at the very point where utmost hatred spews out.

The fundamental notion of *narcissism*—though the term has not yet been uttered—thus emerged in this reflection on the phenomenon of religion. Freud would henceforth maintain, against all odds—against Jung in particular—the principle of the two libidos: one sexual, one egoic, narcissistic, aggressive, each of them meeting with a specific prohibition. The first period of psychoanalysis explored the consequences of this fundamental maxim: "The mother and her offspring will be separated by the prohibition of incest." Its second period set itself the task of exploring the consequences of a second fundamental maxim: "Thou shalt not kill," governing the relations of the individual with his peers, his brothers, and by extension, with society.

Henceforth the antagonistic bond that attaches each individual to the group takes center stage. In moving in this direction, Freud could not fail to encounter the *Halacha*, the object of which is precisely to sort out and regulate that relation.

From the first to the second period, what remains to be elucidated is how, out of the castration the father carries out, respect for the brother can be deduced. Is it a matter of a simple parallelism, as the two tablets of Mosaic Law suggest, or does it contain some secret kernel?

To develop the intuitions sketched in this article about ritual as well as to answer the questions left unanswered, Freud, four years

Chapter 1

later, writes *Totem and Taboo*, with the avowed ambition of solving the final riddle of religion and the group it founds.

The climate—indeed the fashion—of the moment demands as much. Fifteen years earlier in France, Le Bon had published his *Psychology of Crowds*; in Germany, Wundt, a well-known academic psychologist, had attempted to explain the group through individual psychology; Jung thinks he can find in the soul of each individual the cultural archetypes of a collective unconscious. In the equation:

$$\text{subject} \rightleftarrows \text{group}$$

each insists, depending on his inclinations, on one or the other of the two relations. Freud, for his part, wants to grasp their dialectic in *Totem and Taboo*, a key moment in the history of psychoanalysis, marking an attempt at a strategic alliance between his knowledge and that of anthropology, the science of human groups. It was a stormy alliance, which would nonetheless enrich each of the two disciplines, providing the culture with some of its most bracing moments, in wide-ranging debates, such as those that only yesterday brought together Lacan, Lévi-Strauss, and Jakobson. Mightn't today's drabness be due in part to a loosening of this alliance?

What remains to be elucidated is this interest of Freud's in anthropology, this paradox of appealing to the most primitive peoples to explain the most evolved religions and the psychology of modern neurotics.

We need to come back to our premise: "The Oedipal myth is a dream of Freud's, to be interpreted as an evasion." In this respect, *Totem and Taboo* is certainly the fullest exposé of the manifest aspect of this dream—with its ever-after notorious construction of the primitive gorilla killed by his sons who, stricken with remorse, rather than kill off one another as brothers, accept *a posteriori* the law of he whom they've murdered, a construction in which Freud closely connects the two prohibitions against both incest and fratricide. In this dream, ethnology holds a privileged place.

The first lines of the work offer us, perhaps by way of parallel, the start of an explanation of this tropism. "Primitive men," we read, "represent an earlier phase, well preserved, of our own development,"[8] a preservation of the *childhood* of civilization. A comparison is thus being made with the psychology of neurotics as psychoanalysis reveals it, because psychoanalysis underscores precisely the importance of *childhood* in the formation of symptoms. Isn't this an instance of that discursive process that Freud was so taken with, the *gezera chava*, performed here on the term *childhood*? Freud hoped by this signifying transference to take a decisive step toward understanding obsessionals, but also, inversely, toward deciphering the enigmatic origin of religion that merges with that of man.

At the time, ethnology seemed a fully formulated science, considered to have discovered its law of gravity in a key theory, that of the *totem*: the primitive peoples are organized into clans or segments, each possessing a totem, some animal or a plant which the clan members imagine to be their ancestor. Among other things, this totemic principle organizes matrimonial exchanges, exogamy, but also a certain number of rites and prohibitions, such as that of *eating* the totem.

This totemic theory seemed to have reached its state of perfection in 1910, when J.G. Frazer published a weighty, definitive compendium, carved in the granite of observation: *Totemism and Exogamy*. By leaning on this work, Freud thought he could at last answer the enigmatic question: What is a father?

Thus, gradually we come to understand his interest in ethnology.

However, a phenomenon fairly exceptional in the history of ideas occurred here. It is usual, of course, for a scientific theory to age over time, for another to take its place, to spread it by integrating its share of truth. Only totemism, which in Freud's view nothing should contradict, wasn't content simply to age. It was shown quite soon to be, as Lévi-Strauss put it, a "sheer phantasm" that the ethnologists of Europe projected onto primitive peoples. There is no such thing as totemism, but only "the totemic illusion"[9] of the earlier ethnologists. In this, Tylor, Goldenweiser, Murdock, and Boas were right.

Thus, what Freud hoped to build upon as the keystone for his theory of the father proved to be nothing but smoke. Even more disturbingly, the definitive critique of this notion was made within Freud's

---

[8] S. Freud, Totem & Taboo, in *S.E.*, vol. XIII, 1.
[9] Claude Lévi-Strauss, *Totemism*, trans. Rodney Needham (Boston: Beacon Press, 1963).

own lifetime by the authors cited, and at least a trace of this fact enters *Totem and Taboo*. Yet Freud stubbornly refused to take this critique into consideration.

He would soon show the same obstinacy again with his book on Moses, the idea of which came to him on reading the work of a Biblical critic, Ernst Sellin, arguing that the Hebrews killed Moses. Despite Sellin's own eventual public admissions that he had made mistakes interpreting certain Biblical passages, Freud remained unshakeable. As for the totemic illusion, he needed to maintain the same fiction: the real murder of the primitive father. This "neurotic" headstrongness, Lacan suggests, is the decisive element that allows for the hypothesis that *Totem and Taboo* was Freud's dream and must be read as such. This book is the attempt at such a reading.

One may momentarily be surprised that a fact as massive as the collapse of the totemic hypothesis didn't move any of Freud's successors except Lacan to take any stance but an embarrassed silence, in addition to their abandoning the role of the Oedipus complex in their clinical practice. What place, after all, does that shibboleth of psychoanalysis have in post-Freudians' treatments? As we well know, none—with a corresponding loss of incisiveness in clinical practice.

Before undertaking our necessary examination of *Totem and Taboo*, let us briefly look over the contents of other writings by Freud from the same period (1911-1913), to search out the *latent* element contained in the *manifest* aspect of the "totemic dream."

In this fertile period Freud, through the Schreber case, establishes his theory of psychosis, a question that stands in closest connection with our present theme, but which it would be overambitious to take up here. Let me also point out numerous occasional texts, transcriptions of lectures recalling points of doctrine or of technique, and important developments in the theory of obsessional neurosis. We also have found here three texts, disparate in their development but all evidently qualifiable as atypical, if not indeed symptomatic.

The first of these texts concerns "The Significance of Sequences of Vowels" (1911),[10] one of the shortest texts Freud ever wrote, barely fifteen lines. Its object? The divine name in Hebrew, or tetragram (YHVH), of which the Jews suppressed the vowel pattern to the point

---

[10] S. Freud, *S.E.*, vol. XII, 341.

of forgetting it, then substituted for it—as in certain mechanisms of dreams, he remarks—the vowels of the word *Adonai*, "the Master." The tetragram is henceforth legible, once the primitive taboo is circumvented, as *Jehovah*.

The other text is the famous "The Moses of Michelangelo" (1913),[11] a symptomatic text if ever there was one. Freud published it anonymously, or rather, incognito, in his magazine *Imago*, accompanying its appearance with a startling little note: "The author of this article has a way of thinking that bears a certain resemblance to psychoanalytical method." One finds in it the following declarations that no doubt justify the above-mentioned stage makeup:

> Never did any sculpture make a more powerful impression.... I have always tried to stand firm under the hero's angry, scornful gaze. But sometimes I have thus prudently slipped away beyond the penumbra of the nave as if I myself belonged to the rabble upon which this gaze is directed, a rabble incapable of faithfulness to its convictions, and which manages neither to wait nor to believe, but raises its shouts of elation as soon as the *illusory idol* is turned over to it.[12]

The title of the third text would seem to place it at the farthest remove from all this concern with matters Hebraic: "Great is Diana of the Ephesians." Yet here Freud is seizing on a recently published work[13] to venture various reflections concerning Judaism, its schism with the Church, and once more, idolatry. Ephesus, in fact, is a city in Asia Minor that eight centuries before our era, worshipped a mother goddess, Oupis. Its conquest by the Greeks brought about the peaceable replacement of Oupis by the similarly maternal goddess Diana-Artemis. A celebrated temple was erected to her, one that Herostratus was to burn down, and which would generate activity in the crafts and a market for idols that made Ephesus a sort of ancient Lourdes.

The sudden arrival of Jews and of Saint Paul in Ephesus would deeply disturb the city. Paul, target of sharp attacks by his coreligionists, would bring about the definitive rupture between Church and Synagogue. Yet, being "too strict a Jew," according to Freud, he could

---

[11] S. Freud, *S.E.*, vol. XIII.
[12] S. Freud, *S.E.*, vol. XII, 342.
[13] F. Satiaux, *Villes mortes d'Asie Mineure*, Paris, 1911.

not resign himself to the proliferation of idols that dominated the city and since he had great influence, the crafts and the amulet trade fell into crisis. A pogrom ensued, organized by the priests of Diana, the artisans, and the shopkeepers, against the Jews and against Paul, to the cry of "Great is Diana of the Ephesians!", a harbinger of the sinister "Death to the Jews!" The authorities barely prevented the worst sort of violence, and Paul lost the confidence of his flock.

Consequently, the apostle John,[14] who according to Christian tradition was accompanied by Mary, mother of God, took the Church of Epheseus back in hand. Gradually the Ephesians would replace Diana with the cult of a new mother divinity, the Virgin Mary, still devoting themselves to making amulets, only now Christian ones. Thus the former attachment to a mother cult managed to be perpetuated under a new guise.

These three texts show the presence of a strong current in Freud's thinking turned toward Judaism and its millennial struggle against idols, totems, to which he himself would lend a new luster.

For the critical, close study of *Totem and Taboo*, our interpretative key is known: a step-by-step parallelism of the Freudian and the Hebrew text, a new, inverted *gezera chava*. Its cogency will be proved if the arguments already put forth are supplemented by new ones emerging from the study itself and its hoped-for fertility, which will justify the inevitable arduousness of the approach.

The first essay in the book takes immediate account of the fundamental convergence that in and of itself, perhaps, justifies the psychoanalyst's interest in anthropology. Freud had discovered in his reputedly "petit bourgeois" Viennese clientele that the kernel from which the unconscious emerges is the Law forbidding incest. Well, don't we discover, thanks to ethnology, that this Law, despite its secondary characteristics, extends, without exception, to the entire human species, including the most "wild" among its groups, the most backward? It is precisely by this Law that the individual is indissolubly bound to the group, to culture. All reflection on mankind must inevitably come back to this point: For what strange reason does man take a sexual partner from outside of his family? The biological argument

---

[14] The same John traditionally identified as the author of the *Apocalypse*, a text that plays a major role in the deciphering of our myth.

proves strangely feeble to explain this enigma, which, as it happens, religion covers.[15]

But otherwise, Freud does not dwell on this support he receives, sure of the well-founded nature of his discovery. What he asks of ethnology is not some meager outward guarantee for his discipline, but that it helps him to clear up this last enigma by dint of totemic theory. Letting go of his prey to chase a shadow, he immediately runs into two snags.

If the totem represents the primitive father killed by his sons who covet the women/mothers, then killing or eating the totem would constitute a repetition of the primal murder. The punishment of this transgression would obviously, by virtue of the law of retaliation Freud invokes,[16] be the death penalty. By the same token, an incestuous act that transgresses the first Law must suffer the same punishment. Now, "observation" shows the existence of two different punishments, different at least in the way they are meted out: he who raises his hand against the totem meets with a death carried out against him *automatically*, magically, by the totem itself, without the group having to intervene; whereas he who commits incest is *stoned* by the same group. This heterogeneity, pointed out by Freud, poses a first problem.

Beyond that, what surprises Freud in primitive peoples' conduct in relation to the incest prohibition has to do, beyond their submitting to that law, with their *horror* of incest—*Inzestscheu*, according to the title he gives the chapter—prompting them to reinforce the prohibition well beyond genuinely incestuous relations. In our civilizations, only a tiny number of partner types are definitely considered forbidden: mother, sisters, daughters. The exogamous laws of primitive man, on the other hand, oblige him to rule out at least half of the women—if his group is organized into matrimonial halves—and often well beyond that. The primitive would thus have multiplied the guarantees against any risk of incest by widening the circle of interdiction, building a veritable hedge about it.

These two difficulties relate precisely to two cardinal points of the Jewish *Halacha*, which starts out by establishing a protection of

---

[15] C. Lévi-Strauss, *Totemism*, trans. Rodney Needham (Boston: Beacon Press, 1963).
[16] Wrongly.

Biblical interdictions of the same type as the primitive's, aiming to construct what the Talmud calls a *seyag*, a hedge around the Law.

The two different ways of executing a guilty man in turn directly correspond with Jewish legislation. Every grave offense against God is met with *karet*, literally, "severing" or curtailment, with God himself meting out the sentence—a whole Talmudic treatise, *kritout*, is devoted to this. On the other hand, the crimes against the social body, adultery in particular, are punished by *skela*, stoning.

* * *

The second essay of *Totem and Taboo* concerns taboo; it is dense, complex, and the longest in the book. From the very first lines of the essay, Freud himself specifies that this Polynesian term is close to the Jewish notion of *kadosh*, generally rendered as "holy."

This text picks up and develops the theses contained in the article comparing religious and obsessional rites. Undoubtedly it represents Freud's most minute fine-tuning of theory concerning obsessional neurosis, in parallel with that strange religious behavior toward certain objects, people, and situations, called taboos: the faithful person placed near a taboo body attributes to it a mysterious force or *mana*; his fear resembles that of some infection by contact, an unmotivated, absurd fear, like the Kantian categorical imperative, as opposed to intelligible moral prescriptions.

The intellectual powers of the day (Wundt, for one) thought they could definitively interpret the phenomenon by evoking superstition, the *fear of spirits* of those poor half-witted primitives, of which certain traces were thought to have persisted into our own cultures. Freud, in the face of this demonstration by the "sedative power of opium," again poses the real question: To what psychic mechanism does this notion of "spirit" correspond?

By once more using signifying transference, he injects into the taboo his knowledge about obsession, where the rite, as we have seen, corresponds to the repression of a sexual drive further specified here as masturbatory. The taboo, likewise, must respond by repressing a drive linked to touch, namely *murder*. Several times Freud will unfailingly recall the sixth commandment: Thou shalt not kill. Again we find the opposition set up, and by now fully deployed, of two types of repressed drives, sexual in the case of the neurotic, and aggressive, egoic in the case of religion. The taboo masks first the murderous rivalry of man with his fellow man, his *semblable,* and beyond that with his own image.

Freud painstakingly elaborates this thesis by analyzing numerous cases grouped together under three classifications: the taboo of slain enemies, of chiefs, and of the dead, the last of these providing the key to all. The corpse, indeed, represents the desire to kill as fulfilled. The force of the wish, made guilty by its being carried out, has been projected, transmuted into the mysterious energy of *mana*. The desire to kill, to destroy all peers and thus the whole group, is obviously the greatest social danger. This guiltiness calls for punishment, becomes fear of an avenging return of the dead person, since the loved one—thanks to ambivalence!—has suddenly become, by a strange metamorphosis, a hostile spirit. Who, after someone close to him has passed away, has not blamed himself for some form of negligence? A feeling that really originates in the unconscious wish for that person's death, turned into a feeling of mourning, or on occasion, into pathological melancholy.

The taboo neutralizes the violence of similar feelings, metamorphosed into this substitutive and final product, repulsion, the feeling of a radical *impurity* attached to the corpse, *the source and principle of all impurity.*

This chapter definitively underlines once more the importance of the fraternal complex in the phenomenon of religion, a prosthesis for social entropy. It takes the important new step of propounding the notion of the *impure*, derived from the corpse. Even its literary form calls for certain observations.

In this long chapter, Freud enlists an enormous array of ethnological facts, gleaned from all four corners of the globe. From one line to the next, we voyage in his company from Australia to America, from Africa to remote islands, with the growing feeling that this strange text resembles an immense patchwork of variegated pieces, stitched together by a scarcely visible thread, thanks to the author's literary art, precisely like certain dreams well arranged through what Freud himself called *secondary elaboration*. Any reader following the meanders of this text might well lose his way here, through a certain dream-like vertigo.

I would therefore claim that the implicit thoughts of this patchwork concern Judaism, and that Freud's recourse to ethnology constitutes the *metaphor of Judaism*.[17] It would be possible to show step by step, indeed line by line, that these disparate examples—Bantu, Motu-motu, Dayak, Maori—function like algebraic letters relating, by transparent transformations, to the categories of Jewish *Halacha*. The task would clearly be a thankless one, and we must settle for a partial yet sound demonstration. And besides, haven't I pointed out that Freud himself immediately drew attention to the parallelism between *taboo* and *kadosh*? Let me add some key reference points here.

With regard to the absurd character of the taboo as against intelligible moral rules, this dichotomy is also fundamental in Biblical and Talmudic space, which opposes the *mishpatim*—or well-reasoned prescriptions such as: "Do not unto others what you would not have done to yourself," in which reversibility of situation suffices to sustain the interdict—to the *hok*, an incomprehensible, unmotivated rule, which includes, precisely, rites related to food.

Freud had the perspicacity to stress the importance of fraternal rivalry in religious sentiment. In light of such teaching, the Biblical prescriptions in the social domain gained new prominence. There is not one of them that does not contain this reminder, up to the prohibitions of usurious lending, where mention of one's brother would appear inessential: Take thou no usury of him, or increase: but fear thy God; *that thy brother may live with thee*.[18] Isn't all of Talmudic legislation, *seyag*, an attempt to expand on this admonition?

When Freud cited the rites tied to the name of the dead, could he not have known how the familiar language of the Jews treats this same situation, accompanying the name of the deceased with a pious formula: *zichrono lebracha*, "may his memory be a blessing"?

Finally, and above all, the central theme of the second chapter deals with *impurity* and the rites of purification. Now, what is all of *Halacha* if not an immensity of texts, an endless reflection on this very notion of pure/impure (*taharah/tumah*), of sacred/profane (*kadosh/hol*)!

By now it will come as no surprise—though then again...!—that the original principle of all impurity in the Talmud, *av avot hatu-*

---

[17] Could such a metaphor explain, in and of itself, the rather prominent position Jews occupy in ethological literature, from Durkheim to Lévi-Strauss, as well as in-Mauss, Goldenweiser, Boas, etc.?

[18] *Leviticus*, xxv-26.

mah or the "principle of principles of impurity," is the very one that Freud rediscovers after a fair amount of ethnological meandering: the corpse.

The very form of the text echoes Hebraic pages. Confronted with its dense character, its digressions and returns, Karl Abraham, well before me, pointed out its Talmudic character.[19] One passage in particular has drawn our attention by its apparently excessive length—or so at least the translators have judged, since they chose to abridge it. Speaking of the Maoris, Freud offers this quotation:

> The chief must not blow on the fire because his breath might pass on his holiness to the fire, which would pass it on to the pot on the fire, which would pass it on to the meat in the pot that was on the fire on which the chief has blown; thus the person *who ate the meat that was cooking in the pot that was on the fire* on which the chief had blown with his sacred, dangerous breath, will die.

Here the usually scrupulous Strachey preferred to boil things down: "The eater, infected by the breath of the chief transmitted by these intermediaries, is certain to die."[20]

No doubt this refrain perfectly illustrates the mechanisms of contiguity and displacement so essential in the rites, be they religious or obsessional. Yet its structure also irresistibly evokes a curious and celebrated Jewish song that is part of the Passover liturgy: "A Kid, a Kid." Let us, like Strachey, settle for quoting just one verse:

> Death came and killed the butcher who had slit the throat of the ox that had drunk the water that had put out the fire that had burned the stick that had beaten the dog that had bit the cat that had eaten the kid that my father had bought for two pennies.[21]

---

[19] Karl Abraham and Sigmund Freud, *Correspondance*, French translation, Paris N.R.F., 1969. Letter of May 11, 1908: "Some days ago, I was captivated in *Jokes* in a singular way by a small paragraph. On considering it more carefully, I found that, in its technique of opposition and in all its composition, it was entirely Talmudic."

[20] S. Freud, *Totem and Taboo*: S.E. vol. XIII, II.Taboo and Emotional Ambivalence, 28.

[21] Some years ago, an Italian singer, Angelo Branduardi, made a hit song of this, "La Fiera dell'Est" [known in turn in an English version as "Highdown Fair" — trans.].

Thus, in both its form and its content, this second chapter has deep resonances with the *Halacha*, that great monument of Jewish ritualism, to all appearances totally absent here.

* * *

With the third essay, "Animism, Magic and the Omnipotence of Thought," Freud attempts to penetrate still deeper into these strange ritual phenomena. His solution seems to be as follows: the primitive peoples have a psychological vision of the world that consists in totally projecting onto the real the internal mechanisms of the psychic apparatus and of the unconscious. By this inversion, the forces of the drive become spirits, souls, able to migrate from one body to another. This conception might have come out of a reflection on death, compared—i.e. conjured away, due to its unbearable nature—to a special state of sleep.

Out of this overestimation of the psychic mechanisms flows a singular technique: magic, which assumes that certain ritual acts have an effect upon the real, make rainy or sunny weather, or ensure the earth's fertility.

Conversely, certain contacts with nature may profoundly influence the psychic mechanisms, *particularly food*. Whence a certain number of *dietary rites* which primitive peoples observe: a pregnant woman, for instance, won't eat the flesh of a timid animal lest it make her child cowardly.

The set of rites is thus to be deciphered by a magical conception of the world in which the force of desire becomes a cosmic element.

Freud obtained this knowledge, this notion of an "omnipotence of thought" with its evident root in narcissism—man as God's gift to the world—by deciphering the obsessional symptom of the *Rat Man*, for whom rites, private sorcery, had precisely a warding-off function.

Yet again, behind these facts attributed to the primitive peoples, there are our own religious conceptions and especially those of Judaism: the persistence of the soul, the metempsychosis that the Kabbalists admit.

We shall soon give full importance to the deciphering of dietary rites. For now, let us simply insist on these rites' magical function: what the sorcerer or the priest links together through performing some earthly act proves at the same time to be linked in the heavens.

What else does the devout Jew aim for in his piety, with full awareness of the significance of his act if he is a mystic, a *hassid*? The world for him is the result of a primordial catastrophe in which the divine "light" has been lost, scattered, buried in the elements of the universe. The goal of his life must be to liberate some of those primordial sparks, to repair (*tikkun*) this disorder in the world, which is first and foremost that of the human condition.

Thus every trait—and let us stress, *every trait*, without exception—attributed to primitives relates to some important theme of Jewish thought, to its mysticism, the ethnological facts functioning like the letters that both veil and mark some feature of our own religions. In the primitive's delirium, Freud seeks to understand the secret of his own religion, of which he will later say, "Palestine has never produced anything but religions, sacred frenzies, *presumptuous attempts to overcome the outer world by means of the inner world of wishful thinking.*"[22]

No doubt this equivalence between Judaism and primitive thinking bears a heavy charge that might discreetly be defined in terms of *ambivalence.*

* * *

The first three essays in *Totem and Taboo*, for all their interest, would undoubtedly not have been enough to bring the work a fame and distinction beyond that of the Viennese master's other excellent works. If *Totem and Taboo* became an event, this was due to its fourth part—an autonomous unit in the work in which the propositions set forth elsewhere are recapitulated. In it, according to Lacan, Freud constructed *the only myth produced in our century*, by linking together four elements that normally belong to different domains.

The first is internal to psychoanalysis, to its clinic. The study of animal phobias, especially the famous case of "Little Hans" (1909), showed the equivalence in the formations of the unconscious between animal and father.

---

[22] In a letter to Arnold Zweig from 1932. He returns to this notion in a number of Freud's writings.

Chapter 1

Surely we must credit this gifted child, at least in part, at the very moment in which Freud was trying to gather together the scattered elements of his theory of the paternal function, with Freud's sudden, passionate interest in totemism, the second element of the construction, borrowed, as we've seen, from Frazer. For Freud, then, there is no doubt about it: the totemic animal is *a metaphor for the Father*, the mythic ancestor of the clan.

From this filiation we can deduce—but how?—this feeling of the members of the clan, beyond individual particularities, of *sharing a mysterious common substance*, a mystical ether: this feeling they have of being of one "blood."

This sentiment, apparently irrational, is obviously not exclusive to "primitives": it is what cements every human group. We know, from Freud's own admission in the preface to the Hebrew edition of *Totem and Taboo*, that he himself had a similar feeling about Judaism, while also acknowledging his helplessness to account for the inner workings of that feeling.

Among the totem's attributes, Freud notes its being the *guarantor of truth*, the figure before which one makes a pledge, especially in matters of paternity, and the one which presides over *ordeals*.

At this moment, then, Freud finds himself concerned with the question of the ordeal or judgment of God. It seems to enter into his reflection by way of his labors over the book of a famous madman, President Schreber. A tiny detail in this narrative of a psychosis leaps out at him: Schreber claimed, after his recovery, that he could gaze directly at the sun, "the paternal symbol."[23] This is a power Antiquity attributed to the eagle, which would put its offspring to this test. Every eaglet unable to bear the ordeal proved to be illegitimate and was put to death. This myth served as a model for the many peoples that subjected its offspring to similar trials, whether by water, or a totemic serpent's venomous bite, etc.

This important connection between *Totem and Taboo* and the book on psychosis confirms the essential question we are touching on here: What is a father? What is filiation?

An essential question already in one regard: the truth—Freud teaches us in *Moses and Monotheism*—which, *a priori*, doesn't seem

---

[23] S. Freud, postscript to the Schreber case (1911), in *S.E.*, vol. XII.

to dominate practices of human beings, whose every action even tends to conceal it, through this question of the father, always conjectural, plagues man like a permanent thorn in his flesh.

Halacha—but should this surprise us by now?—is quite familiar with this question of the ordeal precisely in relation to the suspicion of a woman's unfaithfulness and thus of filial illegitimacy. The Bible refers to this trial as *sota* and the Talmud devotes a whole thick treatise to it. A look at this trial, however cursory, is important to the pursuit of our topic.

The peculiar rite of *sota* took place only in the ancient Temple at Jerusalem. It consisted mainly of putting a manuscript into a bowl filled with water—a manuscript on which the high priest had written certain Biblical formulas entering on the divine Name—until the writing was obliterated. After this the woman under suspicion would drink the liquid and the writing. If innocent, she would emerge unharmed from the trial; if guilty, she would magically die from it.

And here we see that Freud, in examining the various theories of totemism, notes that of a certain Julius Pickler, for whom the different totems of an ethnic group should be considered as a pictogram, as *primitive writing*.

This shadowy dialogue between Freud and *Halacha* apparently continues when Freud states that the totem is transmitted *matrilineally*, a peculiarity shared with Judaism, which in this aspect constitutes an exception among the monotheistic religions. Is the veil of *méconnaissance* being torn here? Alas! Freud prefers to abandon the suggestion of Pickler, who suits him no more than did any of the other theorists of totemism— nominalists, sociologists, psychologists. None of them seems to have the solution to the questions he's posing: Why the totem, why religion, why exogamy? Investigation winds up in a theoretical desert—one partly of his own making—and in an *absolute enigma*. To resolve it, Freud finds himself forced to make a leap. Hasn't he made other leaps before, and productive ones at that?

This leap, the third element in the construction of the myth, is recourse to one of Freud's favorite authors, Darwin.

By comparing the habits of large mammals—gorillas, horses, cervidae—Darwin had inferred that the first human groups were made up of small hordes led by a tyrannical old male who reserved the women of the group for himself alone. But eventually some robust young male would contend for this chief's position. He would enter

Chapter 1

into mortal conflict with the old male, but then also with every other rival, until he in turn would be chased off or put to death by someone stronger than him. Freud takes up this Darwinian conception and puts it to his own use.

It is pointless to look here for any correspondence whatsoever with Judaism. None exists. Here we can without a doubt pinpoint the moment at which Freud loosens the moorings that have bound him thus far; curiously, this may be the only moment in the whole of his work in which his thinking simply veers out of control.

With seeming serenity and self-assurance, he strides out to encounter this Darwinian thought. The long march of the first chapters is like some painful labor of mourning against this "plague brought out of Egypt." A genuine departure might have led him toward new themes, somewhere beyond the *Halacha*, with no return.

But it surely was just a question of a wrong exit that would lead him straight on to writing a book on Moses. That's not how we slip out of the knot that structures the unconscious Freud discovered. Nor, for that matter, is it necessary to go so far; this *Halacha* slain a hundred times and a hundred times revived, already directs our ear in the fourth and final element in the construction of the myth.

The source to which Freud has recourse this time is a certain Robertson Smith, a specialist in Semitic religions. We owe to this author a theory that locates the basis of these religions in animal sacrifices performed on an altar, followed by the communal consumption of the animal sacrificed. From this convivial act would come the enigmatic feeling that we are endlessly alluding to of sharing a common substance.

In support of this strange theory which was unanimously rejected, to Freud's great ire, by the best anthropologists, Marcel Mauss alone may offer up a meager shred of scripture attributed to the obscure Saint Nilus, an anchorite in the Sinai Desert at the dawn of Christianity, who tells of a rite practiced by the pre-Islamic Bedouins: before sunrise, while Venus was still shining, a camel would be bound to an altar, then slaughtered in a ceremony, sacrificed, and in a matter of seconds, its blood and the flesh off its bones devoured raw by the pack of the devout.

This recourse to Robertson Smith's theory of the *totemic meal* can be criticized on more than one count, and the most eminent ethnologists actually made these critiques long before us. Yet let me add

From the Law of the Father to Fraternal Respect

certain remarks here in line with my argument: Was there any need for such a detour in order to establish how important a place sacrifices occupied in Semitic religions? It would have been enough to open Leviticus, or run through the innumerable Talmudic and Midrashic commentaries that accompany it, to gather infinitely more precise information about these sacrifices, about their link to human nourishment, about the rites that transform each table into an altar.

In Smith, furthermore, the feeling of being of a "single blood" has to do with the group's swallowing of the animal's blood. Yet Jewish sacrificial ritual consists in strictly eliminating any consumption of blood. If we claim that an earlier phase of these religions included ingesting such blood, how might we then explain the later phase that excluded it while preserving the sacrifice itself; how, above all, are we to understand the final phase of the Jewish religion, which totally renounces all sacrifice, yet without the feeling of community lessening (in fact, quite the opposite)?

Rejecting all criticism, Freud thus manages to set in place the four elements of the myth (figure no. 1) he can then enunciate.

The prehistory of humanity would comprise two phases.

The ancestors of humans were originally organized into a horde, a jealous male possessing all the women and chasing out the boys as soon as they opposed him as rivals. This first phase, Freud acknowledges:

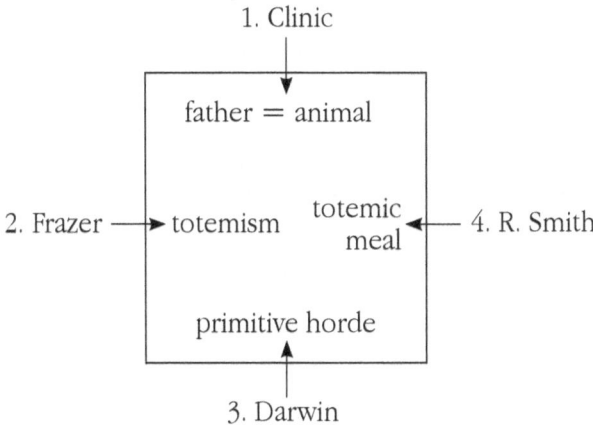

Figure no. 1

was never observed, as opposed to the second phase, that of the groups of male equals subjected to a totem. How did the passage from one phase to another occur? To fill the hiatus there, Freud introduces a reconstruction, a method familiar from the study of phantasms: one day the expelled brothers banded together in a federation, a syndicate, and murdered their father. The courage each of them lacked individually they found collectively. Being cannibals, they ate him, hoping thereby to assimilate part of his strength.

Only, the hated father was also admired. Once Death had allayed their hatred, there lingered, on its own, an all-powerful affection expressed in remorse. From now on the sons, in deferred *obedience*, would forbid themselves what their father in his lifetime refused them. The father becomes stronger dead than alive. Under the Law of exogamy, the men renounce women, who are free now, and thereby create at the same time a pact among themselves. From this memorable act arises social organization, morals and religion—in a word, humanity—born in the blood of the Father-God's murder.

Religion in particular is thus entrusted with the mnemic task of perpetuating, in veiled fashion, the memory of that initial act of achieving a complex compromise between love and hatred of the father, rivalry, and brotherly solidarity. This complex finds its realization precisely in the totemic meal.

Such is the dramatic schema Freud constructed, which has since become a cultural warhorse. No need to recall that the tripod that gave him a support for it is sheer illusion. In his very formulation he reveals a deep deficiency: *What role do the women play here*, even in the earliest phase, the time of the omnipotent master of the horde? Has anyone ever known of a master who didn't immediately arouse *at least one hysteric*? What can be said, then, for the second phase, in which the liberated women-and-mothers become total mistresses of the game? The objection didn't escape Freud, who confesses with his usual honesty, "I cannot suggest at what point in this process of development a place is to be found for the great mother-goddesses who may perhaps in general have preceded the father-gods."

This myth reveals an even graver difficulty: Freud notes in the only "known" example of a totemic meal, that of Saint Nilus', the presence of a divinity, namely Venus, who herself participates in the meal. Wasn't it our belief that the totem-animal represented precisely the divinity? Here then, again, at the end of a work entirely devoted to the question of religion, Freud declared, "the concept of God had emerged—from some unknown source—and had taken control of the whole of religious life."[24] *The enigma of God reappears at the very point where it was thought to be deciphered.* It is a small gain at the end of a considerable effort that peters out in a fiasco.

Built on clouds, *Totem and Taboo* doesn't even lead to a satisfying imaginary construction. Yet Freud doesn't hesitate to offer us this construction, brimming with improbabilities and contradictions, as one offers up one's *dream* to some attentive listener.

Outside of this oneiric field, *Totem and Taboo* today, in terms of theoretical rigor, is nothing but rubble. Can we rebuild a theory of the paternal function on its true, symbolic ground out of that rubble, out of certain intuitions and signifying elements they contain?

Our attention will fix on this cornerstone: identification with the father through his incorporation/ingestion (*incorporation*), operating within a religious ceremonial, the totemic meal. In these wild imaginings of his, what force propelled Freud if not the echo of the Jewish *Halacha* that gives pride of place to dietary rites? It is here that the path toward deciphering is clearly marked out.

---

[24] S. Freud, *Totem and Taboo: S.E.* vol. XIII, 149.

CHAPTER 2

THINKING WITH ONE'S TEETH

Freud's oeuvre, when compared with the great philosophical systems, especially the German, proves to be of different build. It has nothing of the systemic character we find in the analysis of a great body of thought such as Kant's or Hegel's—where the concepts all link up into some grand play of construction. Rather, Freud's writings, open on all sides, give their reader the sense of some dense *fabric*, a weaving in which, at moments, we notice a knot that brings together and sends out threads that branch into some vast expanse.

We shall make it our task to demonstrate that the notion of a totemic meal (which, for all its wrongheadedness, strikes us as the most dazzling intuition from *Totem and Taboo*) follows a thread that runs from one end of Freud's writings to the other: the oral drive. We see this thread emerge at unexpected moments in the development of his thought, clearly signifying—as though that were necessary—that it isn't humbly inscribed only in the register of nutritional need but rather in that of human sexuality, which is structured by a dialectic between demand and desire.

Without claiming any sort of exhaustiveness, let us cite some of the key moments in which orality emerges in Freud's text in its primordial role.

In one of the very first texts of psychoanalytic thought, the "Project for a Scientific Psychology", Freud makes the breast the primordial *lost object*, that which, through its essential property of being lost, provides the first structuring of psychic reality—the conditions that help lead, in the form of the cry and the mother's words, to the conditions first for language acquisition and then for thought. Thus, to our initial question—From where does language come to man?—Freud contributes a fairly weighty element of response: through man's relation to the breast as a lost object.

Rich as it was, Freud refused to publish the text of this Project or "Draft" (*Entwurf*). Yet throughout his life he would return to its main elements. His discoveries concerning the oral drive are set out in the book *Three Essays on the Theory of Sexuality*, which appeared in 1905, but which he would ceaselessly rework in further editions. It is in the 1915 edition, contemporary with *Totem and Taboo*, that we find this addition:

> We will give the name of pregenital to the organizations of the sexual life in which the genital zones have not yet assumed the predominant part .... The first of these is the pregenital oral sexual organization or, as it might be called, the *cannibalistic*. Here sexual activity has not yet been separated from the ingestion of food.... The sexual aim consists of the incorporation of the object, *prototype of a process that, in the form of identification, must subsequently play such an important psychological role.*[25]

This evocation of identificatory mechanisms will be picked up again five years later, in 1920, in his book *Group Psychology and the Analysis of the Ego*, which contains an essay on "identification"[26] whose first lines are central to our present concerns:

> Identification is known to psychoanalysis as the earliest expression of an emotional tie with another person. It plays a part in the early history of the Oedipus complex. A little boy will exhibit a special interest in his father: he would like to grow like him and be like him, and take his place everywhere. We may say simply that he takes his father as his ideal. This behavior has nothing to do with a passive or feminine attitude toward his father (and toward males in general); it is on the contrary typically masculine...
>
> Identification, in fact, is ambivalent from the very first; it can turn into an expression of tenderness as easily as into a wish for someone's removal. It behaves like a derivative of the first, *oral* phase of the organization of the libido, in which the object that we long for and prize is assimilated by eating and is in that way annihilated as such. The cannibal, as we know, has remained at this standpoint; he has a devouring affection for his enemies and only devours people of whom he is fond.

---

[25] S. Freud, *S.E.*, vol. VII, 198.
[26] ibid., vol. XIV, ch. 7: "Identification."

The issue at the core of *Totem and Taboo* is obviously in the background of this text that, as such, for all its straightforwardness, raises a fair number of questions.

For a start, there is the enigmatic Freudian axiom of a first love for the father, or, more enigmatic still, that love is only for the father. We can turn this proposition around every which way, without anything seeming to justify it, yet still it remains vital to clinical observation.

Furthermore, what is meant by this identification called primordial, and which operates as the devouring of the father? How are we to understand it, since no one, on evidence, has ever eaten his father except in the tale of the totemic meal, and some cannibals?

Surely other important Freudian concepts—castration, for example—are equally "improbable" and should be understood within a play of signifying equivalence: the separation from the mother, in the latter case. For the devouring of the father, Freud tacitly refers us to his *Totem and Taboo*, the illusory nature of which we sufficiently demonstrated. And so?

No psychoanalytic author seems to have asked himself these dangling questions. Or none except Lacan, who made these few pages on identification the basis for an entire year of his teaching. What does he teach us about this primary identification?

Apparently very little—for, deliberately, Lacan declares that he will refrain from discussing it, though he gives his reason for doing so. If, in effect, primary identification "[having] emerged first in psychoanalytic experience is of massive clinical presence and a veritable backdrop to every cure", then approaching it remains almost impossible.

His effort, then, will be devoted to the second form of identification, called the "single trait"[27] placed at the origin of writing. But before abandoning the question to any successors who might care to take it up, Lacan indicated a path for research: the privileged investigatory terrain for understanding identification with the father is, in his view, that of the Semitic religions. These few words, if taken seriously, would truly reverse the trend. Generations of Freudians had desperately tried to advance on the side of ethnology and ended up getting nowhere in the study of primitive or "shamitic" peoples. Lacan, meanwhile, hints: Check out the Jewish side instead!

---

[27] Strachey's translation of *einziger Zug* [trans.]

Chapter 2

Freud, by small strokes, produced another famous concept, that of the *superego*. Ever since his first works, he guessed the importance for the psyche of the sentiment of guilt. His article on the rites led him to present the paradox of an "unconscious conscience" embodying remorse.

Starting with his 1917 analysis "Mourning and Melancholy," the idea is put forward that the superego is narrowly related to the oral drive and its aggressive dimension.

This concept of the superego, apparently one of the simplest to understand, nevertheless poses some of psychoanalytic theory's thorniest conundrums.

Freud defined the superego as the heir to the Oedipal conflict, the interiorization of the paternal agency, at the same time that he connected it to the oral drive, the most "archaic" of psychic agencies. A diachronic conception would thus situate the two principal moments of its formation, one before the establishment of the Oedipal rivalry, the other after.

This conception has led to many differences among psychoanalysts, depending on which of these moments they laid stress. Some even posited the existence of *two* superegos, one maternal or pre-Oedipal, the other post-Oedipal.

The second difficulty strikes me as more extensive. The superego, or moral conscience, manifests itself to the subject through commandments, words—in short, in a mode of language. If, on the other hand, we posit that it begins with orality, by what strange transmutation, what alchemy, does the dietary object become an order, an imperative?

This new paradox did not escape Lacan, who, being the peerless reader of Freud he was, came up with the following premise: In the formation of the superego, *the subject swallows words*. How are we to understand such a phenomenon? Lacan never got to articulate this, leaving the question open, as he later would that of primary identification, revealing perhaps that all these difficulties converge toward a single point not elucidated, indeed impossible to elucidate given the state of theory at that moment.[28]

---

[28] Jacques Lacan, *Le Séminaire, Livre IV: La relation d'objet* (Paris: Éditions du Seuil, 1994).

In 1925, Freud would write an article as short as it was dense: "Negation," seemingly far from our subject which can yet shed light on it. What is defined in these pages, picking up on the earlier developments of the *Project for a Scientific Psychology*, is nothing less than the emergence of thought; and since we think only through language, Freud posed the same question as we do: How do thought, and therefore language, come to man?

Thought, this article asserts, emerges only with the appearance of negation, starting from the moment in which, within the continuum of the world, certain objects are affirmed, introjected, while others are rejected.

> The attribute to be decided about may originally have been good or bad, useful or harmful. Expressed in the language of the oldest—the oral instinctual impulses, the judgment is: 'I should like to eat this,' or 'I should like to spit it out'; and, put more generally: 'I should like to take this into myself and to keep that out.'[29]

The first steps of thinking, the primordial structuring, are to be deduced from an initial relation to the oral object. We might best formulate this principle through an image: before all else, *we think with our mouths, with our teeth*. This sets up the basic opposition *good/bad*, which at once entails that of *interior/exterior*.

What is the culture of a group if not the defining of an inside by means of something outside the group: Greek versus barbarian, Jew versus goy, Christian versus infidel?

The culture of a group shows its origin to be in line with the intuition of the totemic meal: orality, dietary rites.

In "Negation," Freud, who paid no heed to the warnings of the first structuralists against totemism, adopts a schema that anticipates their assertions:

> The animals of totemism cease to be, only or above all, feared, admired or coveted creatures. Their sensible reality gives signs of notions and relation, conceived by speculative thought starting from the data of observation.... The notions of opposition and of correlation, that of the oppositional pair (*couple d'opposition*), have a long history.

---

[29] S. Freud, *S.E.*, vol. XIX, 236-237.

Chapter 2

In this brief survey of Freudian references to orality, let us hold fast to the bond that unites this drive to the Oedipus complex through the shift required by primary identification.

Among Freud's pupils, Karl Abraham was the one most attached to this theme of the oral, but also to the psychology of religions—two questions seemingly with no direct interrelation yet which study often brings together. We are indebted to him for important works on melancholia in relation to orality, various writings that anticipate Freud's speculations on Moses. He also intuited the importance of dietary rites and urged their study. Finally, through this two-fold inspiration, he influenced his two most distinguished students, Theodor Reik and Melanie Klein.

Reik, with considerable talent, extended Freud's totemic theories in a set of studies on Hebraic rituals, "Kol Nidre" and "The Shofar," devoted to holiday of *Yom Kippur*.

Isn't it remarkable that Reik, like Abraham, in following the trails of *Totem and Taboo*, immediately enters Jewish terrain, anticipating my reading of the work as a metaphor—albeit a failed one—for Judaism?

In his "Kol Nidre," Reik seems worried about the sort of impasse to which totemic theory leads and attempts to construct a new outline, close to the Biblical text, around the Hebrew term of *Brith*—alliance, pact, contract written both in the Book but also written on the body by circumcision—and that links two parties: God to his people, the Father to his sons.[30]

This contract under oath involves fidelity and mutual testimony by the contracting parties, and lays out what sanctions will befall the group if it breaks its word.

The feeling of belonging to the group comes through a certain number of subjects submitting to the same contract and transmitting it to their descendents.

Reik's schema seems modest in comparison to the grand tragic fresco of *Totem and Taboo* and not up to the task of deciphering the religious phenomenon. But at least it has the merit of being faithful to the Biblical texts and to the subjective experience of the believer. Furthermore, it has all the merit of a project that leaves unbridled speculative vertigo behind, in order to establish itself on its true terrain: of the

---

[30] Circumcision and its ceremony are still referred to as a *bris*. [trans.]

symbolic and the writerly. Its main deficiency in construction comes from the omission of any consideration of orality.

Karl Abraham expresses reservations[31] about this text: the absence of references to totemism, a poor methodology that amounts to obsessing over the holiday of Yom Kippur without taking into account the essential mechanism behind the rite: displacement. It would be better, argues Abraham, to take an interest in the rites preceding the holiday—sound advice, as we'll see, though one can turn the critique against its author, who's content to examine a rite practiced on the eve of Yom Kippur, consisting of sacrificing a chicken—and *voilà*, we at last have the totemic animal we've been waiting for!

Reik will published a second article, "The Shofar," which on the precise point of totemism rides into the very rut his preceding study sought to avoid, that of *totemizing* Judaism, a grotesque effort in which there is a proliferation of totems.

This effort at totemization leads only to definitively privileging secondary, anecdotal rites, such as Abraham's chicken, rites of an individual and not a communal character, thereby neglecting the rich, complex rituals in which this community dimension comes into the foreground.

The great fascination of these authors touches on the sacrificial rites of Jewish antiquity. Who, after all, would underestimate their importance? Yet it is worth reminding ourselves that a psychoanalyst's main interest is neither ethnology nor ancient history. His task is to understand *current* mechanisms through which a personality is constituted in its psychic agencies and its conflicts. No sensible person would claim that the sacrifices of horned beasts in ancient Judaea contribute decisively to this. If the Pharisees, those giants who founded Judaism as we know it today, did away with sacrifice at the very moment in which they were putting into place institutions and rites to ensure the perpetuation of the Jewish people and the sentiment that gives it its strength, one must assume that they did not regard it as irreplaceable, and that through those sacrifices, some more fundamental mechanism was at work, and that one could from that point on, by preserving only that mechanism, forego the streams of animal blood.

---

[31] Karl Abraham, *Selected Papers on Psychoanalysis*, (London: Karnac Books Ltd., 1988).

Chapter 2

Let us recognize in the Pharisees' reforms a formidable efficacy after the experience of a millennial exile—an efficacy in contrast to which the attempt to give animal sacrifices a leading role appears terribly obsolete.

These criticisms having been made of the efforts of Abraham and Reik, we recognize in their works, among these other merits, a deep intuition: the totemic theme overlaps with Judaism, or to be more precise, is directed toward the rites surrounding the festival of Yom Kippur. To be sure, we see them groping about as if in a game of blindman's buff, eyes blindfolded in pursuit of an enigma, one telling the other, "You're getting hot, you're nearly there." They seem to have the foreknowledge they've found the spot to dig at.

We should lastly mention that other great figure of psychoanalysis, Melanie Klein, who, without directly committing her research to the question of religion, contributed to it by shifting it through her labors onto the child and orality.

Klein, in her analyses of very young children, made an important discovery, a profound modification of Freudian theory, that of the early Oedipus complex: as soon as one approaches it, the child reveals a problematic linked with the father. Certain American pediatricians pushed the experiment to the point of placing tape recorders by the cribs of nurslings in their first prattlings and confirmed Klein's thesis.

Up to that point, there prevailed a simple, clear conception, a so-called genetic conception, involving stages: the child was thought to achieve a series of stages of maturation, oral first, then anal, and finally Oedipal, which was thought to organize into genitality the first fragmentary steps of the child's sexuality. This program that also included primary identification, acquisition of language and motricity, was thought to take the child around three years to accomplish.

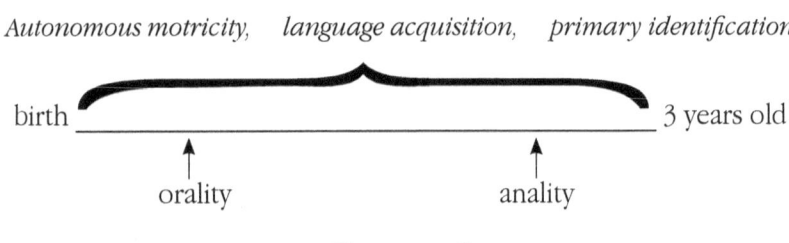

Figure no. 2

Here we see that the Kleinian early Oedipus complex overwhelms, and perhaps fully suppresses, this already short temporal interval. In fact, this destruction bears rather on the plan of stages itself, a first step in the apprehension of phenomena that seems synchronic, moments and places of a structure the little human finds itself immediately plunged into.

Klein's sharp change of direction opens the door to Lacan's conceptions—thereby inscribed in an "Abrahamian" filiation he was nevertheless to criticize quite extensively: the child and its mother never—except in the gravest pathologies—form a duo complete unto itself, but rather a trio in which the newborn quite quickly, indeed immediately, perceives that the activity and desire of its mother, whatever her devotion toward it is, gravitate around something other than the newborn, something fraught with mystery: the phallus.

Thus, there gradually came to dominate in analytic theory—or at any rate the theory we share—a synchronic, structural conception of its leading concepts. Orality is thus no longer merely a moment in the history of a subject, but is ever-present, a particular mode of the relation of this subject to what surrounds him. In the same way, the paternal function, its various psychic agencies, and primary identification, can no longer be understood as brief, unique, discrete acts, but rather as repetitive, on-going and *current* ones, accompanying everyone their entire lives, undoubtedly modifying their place and their respective relations.

Such is the theoretical space in which I want to intervene and propose certain modifications.

PART TWO

THE DISCRETE AND THE CONTINUOUS

Chapter 1

A STRANGE MEAL

With what intuition, what obscure point in Judaism—surely never clarified as such—does the notion of the totemic meal overlap? The enigma lies—as we know thanks to Abraham and Reik, but also thanks to Lacan, and indeed Kierkegaard—in the vicinity of the holiday of Yom Kippur, where the main themes of Judaism converge: the sacrifice of Isaac, the golden calf, purity, expiation.

We shall follow Abraham's advice to Reik, by looking for the key not in the Yom Kippur ceremony itself but in the rites that precede it.

Yom Kippur belongs in the Jewish liturgy to a complex of three festivals. One, Rosh Hashanah, comes *ten days* before it; the other, Sukkoth, comes after it. It has particularly close ties with Rosh Hashanah, the "Day of the Year" marking the creation of the world. The interval that separates the two ceremonies is called *Yamim noraïm*, "days of quaking." The liturgy also refers to Rosh Hashanah as "Day of the *Shofar*," the ram's horn, the sounding of which is constantly heard throughout the day's prayers.[32]

Examination shows that the main theme of this grave holiday is not so much the mythic creation of the world, but rather that of the sacrifice of Isaac by his father Abraham. The event is related, commented on, hammered on insistently, over the two actual days of this "Day of the Year."

The festivities start off with a truly odd culinary rite, the *seder*, a term that in itself warrants explanation. This name is given to the *two liturgical meals* in the Jewish religion, the second being that of Passover; but in addition to this, to the most important of Jewish

---

[32] For the record, the Shofar plays only a minor part on Yom Kippur. It solemnly marks the end of the fast.

books after the Bible, the Talmud, often designated by the name of "six *seders*" or *Chas*. One and the same word can thus refer to a meal and to a book, a parallel all the more unsettling since the term is also (roughly) homophonic with the usual word for a book, *sefer*. In its etymology *seder* refers to the ordering of a sequence, an organizing or layout, a structure.

The instructions for this meal are found in the Talmud[33] and its definitive ritual is established by the master-book of the *Halacha*, the *Shulkhan Arukh*, or "The Set Table" of Joseph Caro[34]—orality and rites certainly converge all over the place![35]

This "meal"—the quotation marks are essential—is attended by the extended family, relatives and cousins, gathered that evening around the family patriarch, before having the actual supper. The atmosphere is grave; a month of numerous penances and prayers (*selichot*) has led up to the occasion.

In the midst of this assembly, which clearly evokes the totemic group, we find a tray covered by a cloth. Could it be hiding the totemic animal that so many generations of analysts have been looking for?

What's uncovered, and where the solution to the riddle truly resides, proves disappointing at first glance. It isn't an animal, but rather *eight* dishes, in small quantity, of which each family member, after pronouncing a ritual formula, is to swallow a small bit: chard, leek, date, squash, sesame, pomegranate, a sheep's head, and a honey-coated apple. This little catalogue makes the enigma complete.

Unless ... the code of this rite is itself concealed somewhere else, close by. As indeed it is—in the formulas spoken before eating.

Asking those who practice a rite what it means has never helped much to explain it. In this case, too, the faithful, if asked, will speak of symbols, of making good wishes for the new year; and indeed some of these elements are contained in the ritual formulas, all of which begin similarly: "That is be Thy will, God of our fathers, that..."

Yet more careful examination of these wishes quickly reveals a dichotomy in their content. Certain ones are "positive": the wish,

---

[33] *Talmud Babli*, treatises Keritoth 10 a and Horayoth 12 a.

[34] *Choulhane Aroukh*, treatise *Kaf Hahayim*, chap. 589

[35] Let us note, however, that today only the Oriental Jews, the Sephardim, perform in its entirety this alimentary ritual that has been simplified to the extreme by the Jews of Europe, or Ashkenazim.

say, that the year be *good*, full of *numerous* happy events. Participants accompany these wishes by eating symbol-foods that present these characteristics: *good* like the taste of the apple, *sweet* like the honey, *numerous* like the sesame seeds. It is startling already to note this strange manifestation of wishes expressed within an eating activity.

Other symbol-foods have a peculiar character. Thus the wish that "... our nation be among the nations at the head and not the tail" is accompanied by the eating of a head, preferably, but not necessarily, a sheep head; a fish head or chicken head will do just as well. What matters is the signifier *head*.

Man's fate doesn't consist of sweet things alone. It is crucial also to envision painful events and conjure them away: conflicts with enemies, natural catastrophes, possible illnesses, events that place death and castration on everyone's horizon. And what foods will accompany the "negative" wishes? Here the notion of symbol-foods totally breaks down: the chard, the leek, the date, the pumpkin, etc. What—shades of Cinderella!—can the pumpkin symbolize?

By bringing in the Hebrew name of these vegetables, we come to the key moment for deciphering this enigma.

NAME OF VEGETABLE	HEBREW NAME	VARIANTS
Chard	*Salk*	
Leek	*Krati*	Garlic = *toum*
Date	*Tamar*	bean = *poul*
Pumpkin	*Krá*	

The first wish in this second category is "that your enemies and those who wish us ill *disappear*." The word "disappear" in this sentence, spoken before eating the chard leaf, is *ystalekou*, from the verb *silek*. We immediately note the homophony with *salk*, the chard.

Under the same conditions the wish is uttered, "May your enemies be *removed*," etc., in Hebrew *yekaretou*, from the verb *karet*, homophonous with *krati*, the leek.

The curse on enemies is bolstered by a third, similar wish: "May they be *annihilated*," etc., or *yetamou*, in homophony—albeit rather feebly—with *tamar*, the date fruit. In certain local rites, the equivalency of sounds has in fact been improved by substituting garlic

Chapter 1

for the date, providing the sound *toum*. Elsewhere they prefer to substitute the bean, *poul*, which allows for a new curse on enemies: "May they *fall*," *yepoulou*.

Finally, a last wish asks God to *annul* any dire decrees He may have prepared against us, *tikrâ*, associated with the pumpkin, *krâ*.

The nature of the procedure, repeated at least four times, leaves no doubt that none of this is coincidental, but a systematically planned effect: *the dishes of the symbolic meal are there only for their names, for the phonemes they contain*. Why, otherwise, would some celebrants replace a date with garlic? *The foods are props for sounds, for signifiers.*

The invocation of death summons up that signifier's sheer phonic dimension. Yet the rite isn't satisfied with the immateriality of the voice; it injects the phonemes into real, material food. Now, a materialized signifier becomes the equivalent of writing.[36] *The food becomes a letter.*

The procedure evokes the rebus or hieroglyphic writing as well as techniques of Midrash. It is completed by the act of eating.

Thus we manage to extract this latent signification from the *seder*: to ingest, to eat words, writing, where, to follow the expression of a fundamental author in these questions, Saint John, "[t]he word becomes flesh and dwells among us." Such would be the true Freudian "totemic meal," this devouring of the father: *to eat writing communally, a founding moment of the group sentiment in a singular cannibalistic act, brilliantly manifesting this passion, love and hate merged, of the human being for the signifier.*

The place of this ceremony in the calendar gives it its full import. This ceremony ushers in all the festivities that mark the New Year. It symbolizes the first act of the creation of the world, or, for each individual, the point out of which his psyche emerges.

In this privileged moment, by incorporating signifiers, man renews the fundamental pact that links him to language.

---

[36] J. Lacan, "L'Instance de la lettre dans l'inconscient," in *Écrits*, (Paris: Le Seuil, 1966). "The Instance of the Letter in the Unconscious" in *Écrits*, trans. Bruce Fink, (New York: W.W. Norton, 2006).

CHAPTER 2

FROM WRITING TO THE BOOK

The phenomenon I have been revealing—the eating of words, the eating of writing—seemed to open up, as though after some arduous climb, a perspective onto a broad landscape comprising both psychoanalytic theory and its clinic but, beyond that, a fresh understanding of the psychology of religions, and of certain enigmatic cultural facts we shall address in due time.

It seemed necessary to go beyond the initial deciphering of a single Jewish dietary rite and to encompass the entire ensemble of Jewish table manners.

We are already warned that man doesn't stand in a simple relation of need to his food; that the *name* of the food, its symbolic attributes play a role in subjectivity that Lévi-Strauss[37] already indicated among the primitive peoples, for whom "natural species are not chosen because they are 'good to eat' but rather because they are 'good to think.'" On this level, all human beings are primitives.

The association of the Word with food is a given of Jewish ritualism. The pious man does not consume even a particle of food, solid or liquid, without pronouncing a ritual formula of blessing, a *brucha*. The word not only precedes ingestion but also follows it, creating a sort of symbolic "sandwich" around everything he swallows. Food is thereby consecrated,[38] sanctified; it changes nature through this infiltration of words.

Furthermore, it is appropriate at the table to exchange bits from the Torah; without them, the act of eating, the sages say, becomes

---

[37] C. Lévi-Strauss, *Totemism*, trans. Rodney Needham (Boston: Beacon Press, 1963).
[38] A symbolic act to be compared with the consecration of the Host, which we shall address later on.

Chapter 2

idolatrous, bestial. This symbolic accompaniment raises the animal act of eating to the level of an activity in accord with human nature.

But the set of these important rites accompanying nourishment constitutes a sort of *external,* superficial application of the word to the flesh; it doesn't in and of itself justify our statement that what is transpiring is "eating of words."

We know that pious Jews don't consume just any food but only that deemed kosher, that is to say, in keeping with a vast complex of dietary prohibitions, the *kashrut,* the masterpiece, and major portion, of the *Halacha*. No devout person will eat a piece of meat, or anything out of a can, if that meat itself or the tin or package doesn't bear a label with the rabbinic seal. It isn't far-fetched to say that this label is incorporated at the same time as the food,[39] though this writing still belongs to an extrinsic relation.

Any attempt to decipher *kashrut* itself, beyond the rites that duplicate it, requires direct examination of its rules. The core of it is set down in *Leviticus*. Yet already it's inseparable from the commentaries, additions, and complications that rabbinical exegesis has contributed to it, a veritable thicket of law-making dispersed over quite inaccessible works: some Talmudic treatises—but mainly the *Hulin*, the juridical work by Maimonides and Joseph Caro, without forgetting the Kabbalistic texts that attempt to explain it. An obviously overwhelming task, then. Quite happily, several authors have already produced a more or less complete compilation. The rigor of our procedure demands having recourse only with those that are "orthodox," i.e. that have remained closest to tradition. Among them I have chosen the clear, handy work of I. Grunfeld, *Jewish Dietary Laws*, which succinctly presents the rules and their main justifications.

Grunfeld immediately sums up the predominant position of Jewish theologians: the laws of *kashrut* constitute the most important element of the Jewish religion. According to him, they have literally "molded the character of the Jewish nation," in accord with the Biblical expression that invariably accompanies their statement: "And you shall be holy as I am holy."

---

[39] This remark echoes with what Wolfson writes in her book *The Schizophrenic and His Languages.*

It's no mystery, then: the main effect expected of the *kashrut* is *psychological*; it forms the basis for the feeling of community in a mechanism of identification. An author as eminent as Maimonides sought to propose other reasons, hygienic and medical, for these dietary laws, but tradition has rejected them, by reckoning that the moral and psychological aspect outweighs every other consideration.

How then do dietary rules possess a moral and psychological effect? The obscurity begins here and it's a dense one, involving important divergences among commentators who nevertheless share the same insight: food has a psychic effect. Don't we know that consumption of certain products—alcohol, drugs, psychotropics—act powerfully on the mind? Why, more subtly, shouldn't *every* food have a positive or negative effect on the psyche? Don't body and mind form a unity? The Jewish theologians affirm this in a startlingly materialist stance. The effect of matter on mind was supposedly *revealed* to men in the *kashrut* as divine, enigmatic, impenetrable knowledge.

We need to recall what we said earlier: *Halacha*, in keeping with the structural dichotomy of Judaism, comprises two types of rules: the *mishpatim*, rationally intelligible laws, and the *hokim*, which reason cannot immediately penetrate. The dietary laws obviously belong to this second class, on the side, oddly enough—as Grunfeld doesn't fail to point out—of those that govern sexuality. Furthermore, the first divine prohibition addressed to Adam and Eve involves precisely the two domains. Man must not eat of the forbidden fruit. Why? Because consuming it will open up to him the doors of Knowledge, and the first discovery that the original couple made after their transgression was precisely that of its "nudity," its sexual nature, with *death* as the first consequence. The dietary laws are deduced through the obscure paths of this primal event. This reflection on "original sin" definitively underpins our present endeavor.

How, in effect, are we not to note the strange paradox: to eat an object involves knowing? Now, does there exist a knowing, and in particular the most fundamental knowing, that of sexual division, of the castration of the woman, that is not *articulated*, constituted by signifiers? Thus the forbidden fruit was potentially writing, which is precisely what we are seeking to verify in *kashrut*.

The dietary laws comprise—as was to be expected, the number *two* constituting the *cipher* of every operation and undoubtedly of

Chapter 2

the whole of Judaism—two parts of unequal importance concerning vegetable produce and meats.

Vegetal *kashrut* seems to be less important. All fruits and vegetables are in principle allowed, the vegetal thus revealing a sort of innocence. Tradition imagines the first man as vegetarian. Only with the Flood, with the rather degenerative evolution of the human species, do Noah's descendants begin to nourish themselves on meat, with first rules setting limits on this regimen. All vegetal species are allowed, with the important exception of produce obtained by crossing species.

To this exception other limitations are added, seemingly minor, yet opening up a path toward explaining the set of dietary rules. They rest on the same principle: a harvest can be consumed only after it has undergone a series of preliminary removals, of first fruits, the tithe, the pontific portion or *terumah* (a gift to the Kohan, or high priest—trans.). This principle runs through every part of ritual: cutting, separating in a continuum a remainder endowed with a sacred status, which must be returned to God or to his priests. This concern for underlining the function of a *remainder*, a lost object for the subject, has multiple manifestations, the best known being circumcision. Perhaps it even can be said that the Jewish people considers itself the embodiment of this consecrated remainder within the human community.

What does this essential rite signify? Lévi-Strauss, starting from other fields of study, has shown that we find there, *statu nascendi*, the emergence of the symbolic, constituted by severing some fraction in a continuous series, transformed into a set of discontinuous, discrete elements. The real world of vegetal foods, riddled with these holes, can enter into a classificatory grid, can belong *intrinsically* to the symbolic order.[40] Eating such foods thus joins the law of incorporation to the symbolic.

With meats, this law attains its full rigor.

The great Biblical reason, which definitively condenses all significations of kosher eating, is the identification through orality with

---

[40] Following Lacan, we characterize the symbolic or language order by two properties: the discontinuous and articulation. The first deciphering reveals the first property, the second is coming up soon.

God, with that Jewish Yahweh who tolerates no materiality, no representation. Isn't there a paradox here, and how does *kashrut* resolve it?

We have long examined the response the first psychoanalysts gave: the Jews eat only certain ruminative animals because, in truth, these were originally their true divinities, their totems. In ingesting them, they identify themselves with them. This thesis raises a host of questions, some of which we have already examined, without even taking into account the whole set of data. For example: Why is this species of fish allowed, and another one not? The thesis neglects the complexity of rites, evades the stern prohibition of all absorption of blood, though it is the totem's very soul and would greatly facilitate the mechanisms of identification.

But above all, this thesis assumes that, in scarcely veiled forms, in Jewish monotheism remains paganism. This response of psychoanalysts thus runs counter to the millennial experience of a people of whom it may be said that its sole underlying reason for being different involves one function: shattering idols. The slippage of Freud and his first students was—and credit must go to Lacan for having demonstrated this—that strange misrecognition of the significance of one of the most prodigious events in human history: the emergence of monotheism. Unlike Kierkegaard, Freud, a Jew, did not want to understand the radical shift of human subjectivity represented by the fictive sacrifice of Isaac, for whom the ram is substituted. Here Abraham manifested the definitive ending of the cult of imaginary animal ancestors. On Mount Moriah, the cult of Ram and its equivalents ceased. The response to the enigma of identification that Jewish tradition contributes stands diametrically opposed to it. But before examining it, let us briefly place it in context.

Meat eating inevitably implies the heavy violence of a murder with bloodshed. How could this act not echo this aggressive force, always about to erupt, so characteristic of our species? It is also fitting to treat this question, as Jewish tradition does, with great caution. This act creates a compromise between violence and remorse.

Is it the trace of this latent remorse that echoes in the great tenderness that both Biblical and Talmudic texts show toward animals? One mustn't separate a calf from its mother in the seven days that follow its birth; a man must never sit down to table before having fed his beasts; the animals too have the right to sabbath rest; one mustn't sacrifice the animals' close relatives simultaneously, or tie donkey and bull together: these are some of the screens that the Biblical text interposes between animals and human cruelty. When the drive reaches points of exacerbation, ritual steps up protections.

It is often overlooked that Judaism considers its rituals particular, without universal claims, attached to its priestly monotheistic function, from which the gentiles are totally exempted. However, it deems indispensable that one dietary law be respected by every man worthy of the name: never to remove and consume any part of an animal still alive. It belongs to the seven fundamental laws, referred to as *noachide*, which all humanity must obey.

In this context, Jewish theology contains a theory of primary identification of a *negative-passive* type: one is identified with the sanctity of God in carefully *avoiding* identifying oneself with the animal, in erecting a screen of rites between oneself and one's inevitable cruelty, in protecting oneself from all defilement.

What we wish to show goes beyond this. A *positive-active* theory implicitly exists in Judaism, completing and supporting the preceding theory. To my knowledge it has never been made explicit. One identifies oneself with God by incorporating this "part" that eternally coexists with Him, through which and in which divine action unfolds: the Word, the Law, the Torah.

To show this, we must, from here on, enter into the detail of the rules that lead from the animal to the kosher cooked dish, rules that at first sight seem inextricably complex. Let us note that they in fact follow certain simple laws.

The first might be called the *historical* or *theoretical law*: *in their broad outlines the meat rites repeat the ancient rules of the sacrificial cult* that took place in the ancient Temple of Jerusalem. Despite its destruction, the *Churban*, the rites perpetuate the ancestral memory of the group.

Lévi-Strauss, following Freud, insisted on this: the rite, whether religious or obsessional, is always supported by a myth, more precisely by a myth concerning the origin that the group claims for itself. The rite is a myth—also a page of History or a legend—but a petrified myth, a "frozen word."

The set of rites and of founding mythology, legends, and real history of a group combines into a discernible memory at every moment of the rite that sums it up, in a place of synchrony, an authority materialized among certain peoples and primarily among the Jews: that of the Book, with its dimension of History.

To eat kosher, then, strikes a chord with this first set of facts of the highest subjective importance.

The peculiarity of Judaism has to do with the impression of this structure not into a simple "symbolic" ceremony, but rather into a ritual fabric that injects the Word into the most intimate aspect of food. It reaches such a point by the second law, a *practical law*, which consists of applying a succession of siftings, of separations into two classes, the permitted and the forbidden. Each stage of this process starts out from a continuum and is fulfilled, so to speak, in a discontinuum.

This operation was referred to already with regard to the vegetal. It is developed fully with meats, where it is repeated a greater number of times.

Among all animal beings, a first massive screening process discards the order of invertebrates, to retain only that of the vertebrates; then, within this order, accepts as permissible only mammals, birds and fish, rejecting the reptiles as an abomination. These first two sortings at once prompt some reflections.

The prohibition of invertebrates—as well as of reptiles, for the same reasons—sheds light on a fundamental trait of Judaism, found again beyond these dietary questions[41]: only the precise object is admissible, defined in its form and its limits, articulated. Conversely, an object with "soft and slimy" character, which presents a fluctuating form, the obvious character of many invertebrates, mollusks, and worms of all sorts, is disgusting—considered the supreme impurity, inferior to that of the corpse. The mode of locomotion of many of these animal species, reptation, relating to the morphological variation we've mentioned, seems to play an important part in this repulsion. All that crawls is called *cherets*. Isn't this the curse that befell the serpent after the sin in the Garden of Eden—where we verify the constant connection of rite and myth?

But why exactly should crawling be a curse? One explanation comes to mind: crawling involves maintaining a close contact with matter, with earth. Freud admitted that these terms symbolized the mother—as the equivocal nature of language directly suggests. Reptation, clinging to earth, appears as the great figure of evil, not necessar-

---

[41] In its legislation of borrowing practices, for instance.

ily of incest, but of fusional non-separation. The deep aim of dietary rites is confirmed as an attempt at interposition, at the point at which the subject tends most easily to come back to his place of origin, of the separating order of the symbolic, contrasting what is erect and desiring with what crawls, and elevation of thought with confusion of thought. Behind the formal grid of a classification, at each stage we glimpse its reasoning, that of desire and of an ethics, a particular tempering of *jouissance*.

These developments seem thwarted by a particular form of invertebrate: the insects. Are they not free of the character of viscosity and adherence, and perfectly defined, aren't they articulated, as indicated by their scientific name of arthropodes? No doubt they are, yet here the articulation, under a form of carapace, is external and not interiorized like a skeleton. Without that, the animal loses the articulated character that is not intrinsic to it, structural, but rather superimposed, so that it becomes similar to other invertebrates. To the aid of these several arguments, not very convincing at first sight, comes a strange exception: one insect among all is considered kosher, a variety of locust or grasshopper which, according to the Talmud, has the peculiarity of having naturally inscribed on its body, thanks to a play of pigmented scales, a piece of writing, the letter *aleph*. This particular case, without great practical importance, has the theoretical merit of corroborating us in our hypothesis: *kashrut* aims to impress writing *into* food. When that writing already exists...

In a new phase, each of the three permitted classes is subjected to a further screening process, chiefly following anatomical criteria—revelatory, as tradition aptly says, of the psychology of these animals—but also following the ways of the species, and for the same purpose: to avoid consuming cruel, excessively "live" animals (Grunfeld), animals manifesting a certain bodily exaltation. To eat them would lead to identifying oneself with them, to privileging physical activities to the detriment of the spiritual.

The anatomical criteria, let us note, serving the separation are always double. Thus, among the mammals, the ruminants are permissible only on the second condition that they have cloven hoofs. The sorting process is thus carried out not only following two characters—the *split* hoof insists upon the dual imperative—but also these are more independent. The permitted animal "articulates" these two irreducible traits by their coexistence in its anatomical unity. It seems to bear the notion of structure as if it were impressed on it. Fish obey this same law of two articulated criteria. To be permitted, they must possess both scales and *two* symmetrical gills. This eliminates all the species with a reptilian morphology—eels, for example—that is slimy and imprecise.

The status of birds is more blurred. Those with the anatomy of birds of prey are eliminated: no beaks or talons allowed. But beyond that a second, rather vague characteristic is at play: "quickness," "liveliness," that is to say, birds with too bright a plumage, or those with great aptitude for flight, able to feed themselves without coming to rest. "Drab," or "colorless" birds—it's tempting to say not very narcissistic birds—basically, those of the barnyard, are retained, since identifying with them does not risk exuberance of physical activity.

When the different species are definitively chosen after three successive sortings-out, the next crucial operation is the slaughter of the animal according to a complex ritual of throat slitting that replicates ancient sacrificial ritual. On a formal plane—to which we give prevalence—it ends with the obsessive action of a new, asymmetrical discrimination: on the one side, blood, and on the other the carcass, a repetition of discontinuity.

The prohibition of blood consumption is exceptionally strict; the precautions to eliminate every trace of it are numerous and precise. Why? Several reasons have been given previously, but it is worth recalling the main one: blood is life, the very medium of the animal's soul.

Tradition insists upon a double danger of this incorporation in that there is an excessive cruelty and abuse of a creature whose soul is being appropriated and whose blood is being symbolically buried. The other danger, by now familiar to us, in ingesting the animal's blood, i.e. its soul, is identifying with the animal. Transgressing the blood prohibition is punished by *karet*, automatic death inflicted by God.

The sacrificed beast undergoes a *post mortem* examination. Any injury to its entrails automatically spells its elimination.

We find ourselves presented, then, with the carcasses of pure, healthy animals, slaughtered according to the rules. Can the devout man consume this meat? By no means! The operations of sorting-out, of separation, are further pursued, intensified.

Already, only the forequarters are permitted—the hind quarters, the most sought after by today's consumers, are forbidden, splitting

Chapter 2

the beast in two. The reason for this interdict is found clearly spelled out in the Biblical tale of Jacob's wrestling with the Angel. The patriarch prevailed, which earned him his new name of Israel, "strong against God." The Angel, on the other hand, dislocated his opponent's hip, leaving Jacob-Israel ever after with a limp.

In remembrance of this crucial event, out of which emerge both a people and a new signifier, Israel, the Bible prescribes a dietary rite: "This is why to this day the Israelites do not eat the sciatic nerve, which is found at the hip joint, because God had stricken Jacob at the juncture of the hip, at the sciatic nerve,"[42] a prohibition broadened for practical reasons to the whole of the hind quarters of the animal. The link between the "mythistory" and the rite is eloquent here: the dietary rite recalls, transmits, the history of the human group concerned in an inevitable reminder, and thereby ensures the group's cohesion.

The remaining part undergoes a new split: the intestinal fats are forbidden. The mysterious reason for this new commandment apparently touches on the essential. Leviticus is content to indicate: "All fat belongs to God," that is to say, the best part, the very substance, rejoining the long series of already carried-out subtractions: *teruma*, first fruits, tithe. This part incarnates in it, as an excess of *jouissance*, a *plus-de-jouir* (surplus *jouissance*), from which one must separate to ensure a regulated *jouissance*, mediated in a cultural order that extols the discontinuous.

To these data, by now secure, Grunfeld adds a new perspective that the psychoanalysts will appreciate, wholly in the spirit of Midrash: intestinal fat is undoubtedly forbidden because of its name, *helev*, very close in its phonetics and spelling to *halav*, milk. Now, we will soon see that the last fundamental dietary interdict concerns the prohibition of mixing milk and meat. This rabbinic author thus confirms our key to understanding: a food enters into a rite first through its name. By not eating it, one avoids incorporating a certain type of bad writing.

The operations of separation are almost reaching their end. There remains nothing more than to eliminate the blood vessels for an obvious reason, and the meat can henceforth be sold as *kosher*.

[42] *Genesis* XXXIII-33.

From Writing to the Book

The housewife, however, must observe a last rite: wash and salt the meat to rid it of any trace of blood before—finally!—serving it to her family.

Here, however, we must pause. The long string of separations seems to us to have moved from one end to the other by the will to create a discontinuity out of a continuum, an essential operation in the passage from nature to culture. Yet won't the rite, for all its persistence, inevitably end up failing in this aim? Mustn't a moment come when the rest of the division will be entirely good, *restoring the order of the continuous*?

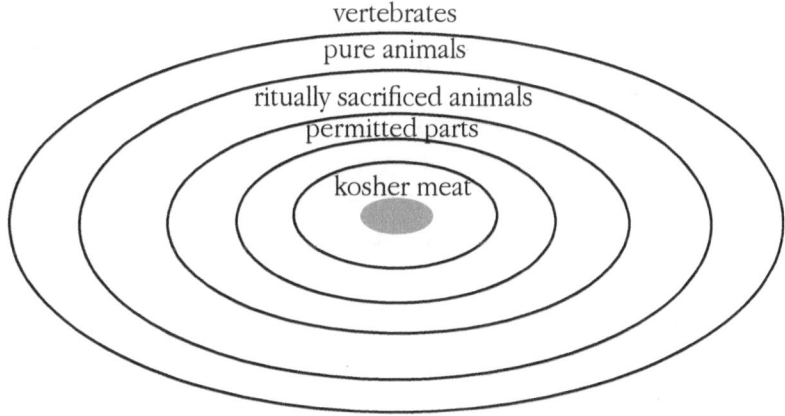

Figure no. 3

Good sense would have it that this objection should be rejected, since it isn't clear how to keep pushing the division indefinitely. However, Jewish tradition reaches this goal by a last alimentary prohibition, perhaps the strangest, surely the most obscure, that governs *kashrut*: the absolute prohibition against mixing *milk and meat*.

Those who are not Jewish will have trouble imagining the extreme consequences of this interdiction. It will suffice to know that no kitchen utensil, no cleaning instrument must be shared for *milchig* (dairy food) and *fleischig* (meat). The precautions to take during a meal to avoid the mixing are imperative. Ideally one would have two different kitchens. This seemingly harmless rule, notes Grun-

Chapter 2

feld, is what gives the homes of observant Jewish their particular atmosphere.

His Biblical reference is found in a versicle repeated three times: "Thou shalt not cook the little one (the young ruminant) in the milk of its mother." The Talmud extended the ban to the order of birds and beyond to a usage that would not be dietary but industrial.

Why this prohibition? The theologians unanimously declare that no man knows why, or, as a medieval doctor, Ibn Ezra, puts it, "The reason for this prohibition has been erased from the eyes of the sage." Nonetheless certain explanations, judged insufficient by tradition, yet interesting all the same, have been attempted.

For the Talmud, milk is simply blood transformed by the udder. The contact of flesh would present the risk of an inverse process. Other interpretations link this prohibition to the whole set of *kilayim*, or a general prohibition against mixing species that are different but with certain properties in common: to weave together linen and wool, to bind under the same yoke the donkey and the bull, raise certain vegetables together, mate animals of different species. Clearly, these efforts seem at once pertinent and inconclusive.

Karl Abraham found this same problem in his clinic and brought it a related answer. A schizophrenic patient—whose religion is not mentioned—could not bear the mixing of milk and meat.

> An association taught me that the taste of the flesh reminded him of that of the milk, that both were 'fatty and sweet.' Similarly, with milk, he might feel a keen craving for meat, which *was as if he were seeking to replace human flesh*. From there, the path of association led to the phantasm of biting the female breast. The articulation of flesh and milk was revealed here.[43]

Abraham seems to be rather quickly satisfied with this "articulation" which Jewish theologians could not resolve over centuries yet which he dispatches in a few lines—undoubtedly of interest.

Maimonides, on this question, warrants particular attention because he offers two solutions to the meat-milk enigma.

---

[43] Karl Abraham, *Œuvres complètes*, tome 2 : 1915-1925 (Paris: Payot, 1989).

The first is medical and dietetic. As a physician he considered a plate of meat and cream quite indigestible, a marginal explanation in relation to the psychological aim of the rite: to shape the personality.

But Maimonides also ventured a second hypothesis, much more beguiling, in which he assumes the link that I have not ceased to underline, between rite and history-myth. If the combination of milk and meat seems so grave, it must touch upon a grave and fundamental question. Now, what is the fundamental aim of Hebrew interdictions? To root out idolatry. One can thus assume a connection between paganism and the mixing of milk and meat. Maimonides inferred from this that there must exist in the pre-Mosaic cults of Canaan a rite consisting of having a small ruminative animal cooked in its mother's milk. The vehement prohibition of this practice institutes a break with idolatry.[44]

Now, this bold speculation has been verified in our century thanks to the archaeological discovery of the Ugaritic writings. In ancient Canaan there did in fact exist a fertility celebration that consisted of cooking a kid in the milk of its mother, accompanied by the usual sacred sexual orgies. One can only marvel at the great Talmudist's insight.

All the same, his response merely shifts the question: Why, in the Canaanite imaginary, could this rite enhance the earth's fecundity? The answer seems clear: in eliminating the prohibition of incest. What, after all, is this prohibition? Lacan excellently formulates it in this way: a double prohibition, on the one hand, it aims at the mother the injunction: "Thou shalt not reincorporate what thou hast brought forth!" and on the other hand, tells the child it must give up desiring its mother. By placing the dead kid "in its mother's milk," in a rite, let us recall, addressed to a mother goddess, the first term of the interdiction is symbolically eliminated.

Whatever the scope of this interpretation may be, it does not exhaust the meaning of the milk-meat ban, the definitive keystone of

---

[44] Cf. *Encyclopedia Judaica*, article "Dietary Laws." This may open up a path for understanding other prohibitions, such as that of pork. One finds another rite of Greek idolatry, in honor of Demeter, the Thesmophories—practiced by women, these consisted of tossing into caves piglets that, once they were dead and spoiled, were mixed with seed and placed upon an altar. This rite, in its signification, is close to that of Canaan.

Chapter 2

kashrut. The formal, structural function of this rite, while encompassing it, goes beyond the earlier meaning.

Up to this point this essential prohibition appears to be isolated in the totality of meat-related *kashrut*. In fact, it is intimately connected to it and completes its system.

We had, in fact, remained somewhat "out of commission" in our analysis of the set of separating operations that ends with kosher meat. A moment had to come in which the discontinuous would be abolished in a continuous remainder if precisely at that final moment, the implementation of the radical prohibition of mixing milk and meat, each one, perfectly legitimate, would not *definitively reintroduce the two*, the alimentary division.

But furthermore, this law finally allows us to go beyond the dimension of the discontinuous, necessary but not sufficient for founding the signifying order. This law introduces the second dimension indispensable to the symbolic: *articulation*. Milk and meat appear as two connected terms in a binary opposition, one excluding the other, following the synchronic law of the signifier.

Finally, this law likewise constructs a diachronic, temporal articulation. Usage, in fact, would have it that a meal, a menu, presents a conventional order: entrée-meat-dessert. Nothing, after all, prevents these terms from being reversed. The milk-and-meat ban creates a compulsory "syntax" in the Jewish meal: the subject may consume milk *before* eating meat, but is not allowed to consume it *after*.

Thus, not only does the mixing of milk-and-meat make the signifier emerge, by materializing it in the food, giving it the status of writing, but furthermore it sets up a vectorialization of time and thereby even an embryo of grammar. *It is no longer words one eats, but phrases.*

We have come now to the end of this structural analysis of *kashrut*. What does it teach us?

First, this confirmation of Freud's intuition in *Verneinung*—that thought emerges, constitutes its primordial categories, in orality and the relation to the alimentary. Judaism pushes these matters so far that it ends up transforming all that it eats, by different yet convergent processes, into an object structured like writing. With the least morsel a Jew eats, before swallowing it, he evokes a whole precise classificatory grid, he secretly performs a sort of chemical analysis: What does this food contain, where does it come from, by what rite has it been prepared?—and on each of these rites there hangs a cluster of mytho-historic facts.

Above all, emerging with implacable insistence, at the same time in form and in significations, is the number two, matrix of all logic: true or false, T or F, 0 or 1. A tension is expressed, through the successive splits, the antagonism milk-meat, so that the minimal opposition is maintained, an overdetermined 2, a 2^n.

In the dietary rites there is a sort of Hebraic *yin-yang*, a gap maintained whose abolition would signify chaos. Through so many rites as well as Talmudic debates the assertion is repeated that the good resides in the precise definition of objects, in the maintenance of discontinuities and differences, in "saying well," and evil in the collapse of differential divisions.

Karl Abraham, who had sensed the binary character of the Jewish ritual edifice, saw in it the relics of a primitive cult given over to cloven-hoofed ruminants: the bull, the ram. Our inspiration would lead, inversely, to posit that the importance of the "cloven hoof" in the sacrifices as well as in the dietary rites has to do with the incarnation of the number two, which it achieves with the emergence of the signifier that this number comes to encipher.

The Freudian thesis according to which every obsessional symptom evolves toward the realization of the wish that it represses, would, transferred to the religious domain, demonstrate that the truth of the Hebraic sacrificial rite had to do with a first approach to what will ensure its preeminence in the Talmud and the Kabbalah: the letter and the number.

Unlike idolatrous paganism, which bred phantasms of fecundity in its sacred orgies, in its sacrifices of children, through a phantasmatic and deathly return to the mother, Jewish monotheism, by its Law of the father, placed this fecundity in the acceptance of the cut, of the signifying division. Thus the domain that analysis of dietary rites opens up is that of the paternal function, which has its hold upon the subject not at an advanced stage of genital maturation, but from that primordial moment that constitutes the oral relation to food, to the breast.

The analysis of one last fundamental rite will enable us to go further, expanding this intuition to its true dimension.

CHAPTER 3

THE BIRTH OF THE SUBJECT

A first step in deciphering the Jewish dietary rites outlined the process of how isolated substantives providing the phonetic root of a verb are incorporated. Next, *kashrut* furnished a vast domain of practices in which the incorporated units kept expanding, were articulated into phrases, and gathered into networks of a cultural group's essential "mythistories." Let us assume now that one last rite will give us the key to the whole edifice: the paternal function.

The Hebraic calendar presents the peculiarity of having several New Year's Days, mainly two. At the end of summer, the cosmic New Year's Day, commemorating the creation of the world: *Rosh Hashanah*, introduced by the rite of the *seder*, which was our "open sesame." Also called the Day of the Shofar, it is placed under the symbol of the ram sacrificed in place of Isaac, or the end of animal divinities replaced by the one-and-only, unrepresentable God.

A second, civil, New Year's Day is celebrated in spring, on the first of the month of Nissan. Two weeks later comes one of the major Jewish festivals, seven days long, from which all the others derive: Pesach, the Jewish Paschal festival, celebrating the exodus of the Hebrew slaves from Egypt and the *birth* of the Jewish nation. Just as Rosh Hashanah is linked to Kippur, Pesach is joined to a second essential festival, Shavuoth, or the Jewish Pentecost, commemorating the giving of the Law on Mount Sinai. The animal sacrificed, symbol of Pesach, is no longer the ram but his offspring, the lamb.

If throughout the year the Jews demonstrate a singular attitude toward meat eating, during the seven days of Pesach they perform even stranger rites involving vegetables, chiefly grains, especially on the first evening of the festival.

On that night, before the meal proper, gathered into an extended family around a patriarch, they have another ritual meal, a *seder*,

Chapter 3

the elements of which are put out on a platter and covered by a cloth. Mightn't this be the true Freudian totemic meal? Once again, the curtains part, to reveal not an animal totem—though a lamb is represented there—but rather a set of quite disparate dishes of which each member of the group will sample a little bit.

Before attempting to decipher this consumption—obviously drawing on our newly acquired knowledge—let us point out a peculiarity of this repast, missing from the rites examined above: the absorption of the ritual elements is inserted like a form of punctuation in *the reading of a specific book for this festival*, the *Haggadah*. The relation to the Book here is no longer latent but manifest, a pivot for the rite.

Haggadah means story, "mythistory," the telling and commentary of the epic of the flight out of Egypt. In a few paragraphs addressed in particular to children, this text tells the story of the Jewish people, its birth. Thus the previously acquired findings are immediately verified and reinforced: the relation of the rite and of the myth, the incorporation/ingestion of the Book of which we cannot tell whether it seized in its structure the foods consumed or whether, conversely, its pages are enclosed in the network of ritual foods—a theme of reflection for an Escher drawing.

But the Paschal rite allows us to go beyond a verification and by essential meanings, fasten onto the interpretation of Jewish rites by examining the foods that give Pesach its character: two vegetable items or their by-products, the *maror* and the *matzoh*.

Maror in fact designates no specific vegetable but rather a category of plants that fall under the heading of "bitter herbs": lettuce, horseradish, parsley and other varieties, depending on local customs. As with Rosh Hashanah, the importance lies not in the signified, but in the signifier *maror*, "bitterness," which one eats remembering the sorrowful existence the Hebrews led as slaves in Egypt.

Egypt ... in Jewish memory this word by itself stirs up deep waves of complex meanings, of which Freud thought he had found the last word in his *Moses*. The Hebraic—or Arabic—term for Egypt, *Mitsraim*, already contains important connotations: "narrow country," the slender alluvial valley of the Nile. This geographical peculiarity has given rise to metaphysical considerations. The Jewish people were established in this narrow place, at once nourishing and noxious, that in homophonic play becomes the locus of all anxieties (*tsara*), perversi-

The Birth of the Subject

ty, incest. *Maror* thus designates this complex Egyptian experience for Judaism, prehistoric and at the same time integrated, incorporated.

The signification of the *matzoh*, an unleavened bread, appears to be much more complex, the major enigma of the entire rite. A first element of elucidation is provided by Exodus XII, associating this *matzoh*, with the *hasty* departure of the Hebrews, who did not have time to let their bread rise. All further deciphering must take account of these first data of explanation, which will soon prove insufficient.

First, a close examination of Exodus XII immediately reveals a contradiction. It contains the commandments dictated by God to Moses, *several days* before the great event of the liberation, among them those that create the obligation to eat the unleavened bread and to sacrifice the lamb. The notion of haste is incomprehensible, the Hebrews having been told well in advance that they would have to eat unleavened bread.

The explanations tradition gives for this prescription will bear curiously not upon the unleavened bread—*matzoh*—but on its opposite, the *hamatz*, a term that designates the leaven or yeast, but also all fermentation, all mold. If prevalence, in regard to a rite, is given to the signifier, isn't it remarkable that *matzoh/hamatz* forms an opposed pair of terms in anagram, a new illustration of the insistence of the laws of language that the rite inculcates in the subject with an explicit violence?

During the weeks leading up to Passover, Jewish houses are virtually turned inside out, that is to say, repainted, with cupboards and storage chests emptied and cleaned, in pursuit of the tiniest bread crumb, kitchen utensils made new, the old ones being, according to certain customs, deliberately thrown away, or at the very least boiled clean. This massive spring-cleaning prepares the home to receive the new Pesach.

The issues of leaven we have been following develop into a rich network of implications, one in which the notion of swelling, i.e. pride and narcissism, features prominently. Related to it is the idea of a "bad principle," a drive which no doubt isn't terribly evil but must be kept in check.

Finally, the unleavened bread presented here as the "bread of affliction" of people racing toward their freedom, appears elsewhere as the exalted or "noble" food par excellence, the food reserved for the priests. The Catholic Church has retained this last lesson in making unleavened bread its Host.

The whiteness of the *matzoh* clearly places it in a vast symbolic grid. But why the imperative to consume it this evening in particular, what signifier and what writing are involved that the subject is made to swallow?

Let us use the lesson to be drawn from the *seder* of Rosh Hashanah: certain foods provide the substantive of their name as the root of a homophonic verb, for example, the bean, *poul*, serving to introduce the verb *yepoulou*, "they fall." Might the enigmatic *matzoh* serve the same function? Consulting a dictionary will immediately answer the question, and even exceed our hypotheses. The same spelling, in fact, designates two verbal forms.

We discover that *matzoh* signifies "to press," "squeeze," as, for instance, juice from a fruit. But also that it is a form of the verb *matsats*, "suck." Thus the unleavened bread would condense two fundamental terms: the dripping or flowing out, as of some overripe fruit, of the people of Israel from its Egyptian containment, as well as the relation to the breast, sucking.

At this point it is necessary to reread the whole of this epic that was the flight out of Egypt. A narrow receptacle in which the descendants of a single man, Jacob, will multiply so much that their presence will prove awkward yet their departure also seem difficult. The body of Egypt subjected to those terrible convulsions that are the plagues,[45] repetitive, prolonged, until the moment of possible expulsion of Israel. Then a sort of calm between two plagues in which any way out seems annulled until a new crisis reopens the passage.

At the tenth convulsion, amid the haste and bloodshed, is produced one of the greatest events in History: the people of Israel emerge. All that remains is to cross a narrow gully, in the midst of the waters of the Red Sea, forming two liquid walls around a narrow passageway. The great battered body of Egypt expels, in trauma, a little body, a new nation, radically different from it.

If this epic has such a deep hold upon the reader, even the non-Jewish one, it is because it represents, with an exceptional vivid-

---

[45] Let us note that these plagues of Egypt—blood, darkness, vermin, frogs, etc.—make up the catalog of classic phobic objects.

ness, a prodigious staging in which the birth of a people reflects that of every little person. Is it any wonder that at this point the first food, this *matzoh-sucking*, should contain an echo of the breast?

This notion is bolstered by the texts of the Kabbalah, in which Egypt is considered the Mother—of all cultures and of all secrets. The Jewish Passover indeed represents the saga of the birth, traumatic as ever, of a human group, in which every person can recognize his or her own birth. Christianity, with its stubborn determination to close the great Hebraic cycle in its own, will stage the other trauma in Easter through death, the complement of being born: dying.

Meanwhile, our own effort isn't quite over. Pesach, we were saying, is connected to Shavuouth. Here there is no alimentary rite in particular,[46] yet the rites of the Passover gather their full meaning only in the aftermath of the Jewish Pentecost, commemorating the descent to earth of the Torah in the form of a mnemonic aid, the *ten sayings* or *commandments*.

Ten commandments: the expression evokes ten imperatives. To our surprise, we count only nine; the tenth—or first—is the simple declaration of a majestic I, *Anokhi*, which apparently has nothing of commandment about it: "I am Yahweh your God, who brought you out of Egypt, from the land of bondage," a phrase repeated in an abridged form throughout the Bible.

Jewish tradition—Judah Halevi, for instance—saw in this declaration the kernel of the whole Torah, which could be deduced entirely from it. This same tradition teaches us to regard the exodus from Egypt not as a historical event at a particular point, but as a *current* one everyone repeats "all the days of your life and all the nights." That is to say, not as some past individual or collective genetic stage but as a structural given.

What would a "structural birth" be and what does this haunting phrase signify: "I am He who brought you out of Egypt," accompanied at times by this exhortation: "You must never return to Egypt"? Obviously the prohibition does not bear on the actual country, where very great masters of Judaism, including Maimonides, actually lived.

---

[46] An inveterate tradition recommends for that day the consumption of *dairy* food!

Chapter 3

Our analysis leads us to decipher the epic and the rites that commemorated it as an allegory, a dream that expresses in a more complex yet more precise version the Freudian myth of Oedipus and its resolution in the Law, the paternal function which is a form of saying—to the mother, on the one hand: "You are not to take your offspring back into you," and to the child, on the other hand: "You are not to desire your mother, who was my desire, you are not to return to her breast, you are not to go back to Egypt."

All that occurs in Exodus, the series of plagues, the pursuit of the freed slaves by Egypt, the Hebrews' nostalgia for their former country, may henceforth be inscribed on the two edges of this cut: "*I am he who brought you out of Egypt....* Your birth is no mere biological process of expulsion or flight. I deliberately had you born as subject to your own desire."

The structural birth repeated with each new day is the symbolic one of the advent of the subject. We have pushed things to this point only to rejoin Freud and his last great work: *Moses*. What I have written, said Freud, is a scandal for my people. In what respect? If there is scandal here, it is surely not in the anecdotal point in which he thought he'd located it: Moses was Egyptian. We have already shown elsewhere that this supposed rocket was a dud. The Zohar goes as far as saying that every Biblical occurrence of the term Egyptian designates Moses, and a number of great masters of the Talmud were converts, including Akiba and Rabbi R. Meir.

Scandal is evident in the work, only it's displaced. Not only does Freud assert in it that Moses was an Egyptian but also that his companions, the Levites, the elite, and above all the Mosaic religion, were also Egyptian.

The Hebrew people and its culture are no more than a bit of Egypt, a pseudopod it issued, pursuing its Egyptian existence beyond its former borders. There is no longer any cut, any exodus from Egypt, or some radical turn of History, there is no longer any place for the fundamental statement: *"I am He who brought you out of Egypt, from the land of bondage."*

We find once more, in a new form, that slippage we noted in *Totem and Taboo*, the neurotic negation of one's own culture. It's a curious paradox: the man who undoubtedly, since the ancient masters, best understands the message, this thinker who reintroduces the paternal function into a bloodless West, is the same one who with his last breath, amid the agonies of cancer, overturns his own teaching, waters it down, even to the point of restoring maternal omnipotence.

We have come—or almost come—to the end of our toils to construct this thesis: the paternal function takes hold of man at birth, from his first relation to the breast. Over the biological activity of nourishment it superimposes the domain of desire, which operates in a dialectical play of demands. The setting up of the structure with its separations and its splits, the identification with the father and, beyond it, with the group, the emergence of the Law which regulates desire, operates far from all totemic errancies[47] in this phantasmatic and real allegory of *eating the Book*.

---

[47] It rather seems to me I've taken up Reik's inspiration about the *Brith*, the contract of alliance, and have carried it to its conclusion: the subject eats this contract.

Chapter 4

WRITING AND FIRE

An immediate objection arises from our preceding exposition: if the operation of *eating the Book*, entirely drawn from Jewish rites, plays the fundamental role we are attributing to it, why should it not be mentioned *explicitly* in the Hebrew texts? As a matter of fact, it is, even if people seem not to notice it in the eminent place it occupies.

We have alluded to the *sota*, the ordeal that briefly caught Freud's attention,[48] and applied to the wife suspected of adultery, who was forced to swallow written-out Biblical verses dissolved in water. The wager behind this divine judgment is clearly to contribute an answer to that most conjectural of questions: "Who is the father?"

Yet we also encounter other strange practices, all of Talmudic origin, this time concerning the child who *is beginning to learn to read*—a detail we should try not to forget. His elders get this child to eat the first egg laid by a hen, an egg on which the teacher writes a formula mentioning the Name. Some touching pedagogical customs are connected to this prescription. In certain communities, the first reading lesson is on a tablet containing certain letters written down and then covered in honey.[49] For the first lesson, the young pupil needn't decipher the inscriptions but simply lick the honey until the writing's erased—which is to say, swallowed, incorporated. In similar practices, the young pupil is served cakes baked in the form of edible letters he has to eat. The immediate explanation for these pedagogical customs—associating a pleasurable taste experience with study, thereby

---

[48] Above, p. 31.
[49] The choice of honey, we shall soon see, has its importance, and goes beyond its flavor.

Chapter 4

displacing oral *jouissance* onto the latter—restored to the domain we are trying to work our way through, seems quite inane.

Our theme is found again in the medieval Jewish legend of the Golem of Prague: a Kabbalist, having successfully penetrated the ultimate mysteries of the creation of man, manages to fabricate a clay statue, which becomes his servant and bodyguard. How does its creator instill movement and intelligence in this clay colossus? By putting in its mouth a manuscript bearing magic formulas. When the creature escapes its master's power, all the latter has to do is take back the manuscript for the creature to revert to mere clay.[50]

Through this cluster of examples, the notion of "eating writing" as the origin of humanization, beyond our own speculations, is shown to be deeply rooted in Jewish tradition. Another instance of this is a Biblical text of great importance: the two first chapters of Ezekiel, who is considered, on the basis of this text, the greatest prophet after Moses.

The Book of Ezekiel opens with a vision, *ma' asei merkaba*, of the celestial chariot or throne of Yahweh. There we first find described four strange creatures, each of which has four animal faces. Then the vision, which literally dumbfounds the prophet, accentuates its fantastic quality until, shattering this mute fascination before a speechless world, Yahweh's voice calls out to Ezekiel, bids him to distinguish himself from his fellow men in their rebellion against the Law, an ecstatic experience for him that we find again in other prophets. Yet what is unique is his conclusion:

> But thou, son of man, hear what I say unto thee; Be not thou rebellious like that rebellious house: open thy mouth, and eat that I give thee.
> And when I looked, behold, an hand was sent unto me; and, lo, a roll of a book *was* therein;
> And he spread it before me; and it *was* written within and without: and *there was* written therein lamentations, and mourning, and woe.
> Moreover he said unto me, Son of man, eat that thou findest: eat this roll, and go speak unto the house of Israel.
> So I opened my mouth, and he caused me to eat that roll.

---

[50] In a variant of the legend, the manuscript is replaced by a direct inscription on its forehead.

And he said unto me, Son of man, cause thy belly to eat, and fill thy bowels with this roll that I give thee. Then did I eat *it*; and it was in my mouth as honey for sweetness.

And he said unto me, Son of man, go, get thee unto the house of Israel, and speak with my words unto them.[51]

A startling text! Yet by no means one whose full implications can emerge on a first reading.

All of Kabbalistic speculation originates in two texts: the beginning of the books of Genesis (*ma 'asei berechit*) and of Ezekiel (*ma 'asei merkaba*), the text we're examining. Esoteric tradition has accorded it extreme importance in summing up in a few lines the supreme mysteries. By now, of course, it seems less surprising to be positing our *eating the Book* as the key to Jewish alimentary rites.

Ezekiel's text has the merit, moreover, of providing new meanings to this fundamental phantasmatic mechanism. It closes a first phase of the vision in which the prophet falls silent. Then a voice, surely that of the Father, rings out and breaks the spell: "*Eat this book and go speak...*" The ingestion of the Book, a rite of initiation, proves to be the indispensable preliminary for the "son of man" to be able to speak. If the Bible represents the place for the emergence and constitution of man's relation to the signifier,[52] its episodes become the metaphor of the main moments in which every subject—you and I—is constituted, which explains the profound impact any reader of the Bible can feel, whatever his origins and convictions. The two moments of the *ma' asei merkaba* seem to provide us with the secret of everyone's history, first of all an *infans*, subjected to language but as yet unable to speak, then acquiring speech. *Eating the Book becomes the mechanism by which the child acquires his language.*

We should once again curb our impatience to draw the consequences—clinical ones in particular—of this conception, in order to deploy it to its fullest, and so gather its richest possible yield.

Deploy it while lingering a little longer within the particularity of Judaism.

---

[51] Ezekiel 2:8-3:4

[52] A conception taken from Lacan. See in particular his seminar on angst, *Le Séminaire de Jacques Lacan, Livre X, L'Angoisse* (Paris: Éditions du Seuil, 2004).

At first glance, in fact, Ezekiel's text seems unique. The history of Israel had to be shattered in Babylonia for the prophet of exile to manage to extract this new theme from Mosaic doctrine. We shall show that it was latent from the first steps of prophetic teaching—and was so by way of *an equivalence drawn between writing and fire*.

The equivalence *writing ~ fire*, highly important and now demanding our protracted attention, is one we can easily draw from Midrash itself, indeed from the first lines of the Midrash Tanhuma, for which the first writing, that of the Law of the ten commandments, was composed of fire: "And the Torah, with what was it written? With a black fire on a white fire."[53]

Eating writing would thus come back to eating fire and thus burning one's lips, a burn that opens them to the act of the word, not without leaving an indelible scar. Who, after Freud, is unaware that the mouth is the privileged place of a burn discreetly referred to as a drive?

The transformation:

eating the book ~ eating fire → lip scar

allows us to find Ezekiel's experience anew in each of the great prophets, however partially.

First in the greatest of prophets, Moses himself, of whom we know through the Bible that his mouth bore an infirmity. Where did it come from? The Midrash, in its reconstruction of Moses' childhood, tells the following tale, close to traditional Oedipal myths: Moses, while still an *infans*, is playing at the knees of his adoptive grandfather, the Pharoah. At a certain moment, to the amazement of the court, he removes the royal crown from the sovereign's head and puts it on his own. The desire is transparent and does not escape those keen experts, the Egyptian magi: to take the place of the sovereign. Forthwith they recommend that the child should immediately be put to death. Yet Pharoah, implored by his daughter, yields to a surge of pity. Why not instead put Moses to a test, an ordeal, which will prove his intelligence and aptitude? Two dishes are placed before him, one with dates, another with live coals. If he chooses the former they will put him to

---

[53] Cf. the translation I gave of this Midrash in my *L'Enfant illégitime*, p. 277.

death; if the latter, they will spare his life. The child puts his hand to the coals and painfully brings them to his mouth, which of course will be burned. His life is saved but he will forever suffer from a "clumsiness in the lips" of which he will later complain in his dialogue, precisely, with the Burning Bush, when it orders him: "Go and speak..."

We find ourselves confronting another great prophet, Jeremiah, again at the start of his message, a brief but precise allusion to each of the themes: the *infans*, incorporation of the signifier as a turning-point in language acquisition, and again, "clumsiness in the lips":

> Then said I, Ah, Lord GOD! Behold, I cannot speak: for I *am* a child. / But the LORD said unto me, Say not, I *am* a child: for thou shalt go to all that I shall send thee, and whatsoever I command thee thou shalt speak.... Then the LORD put forth his hand, and touched my mouth. And the LORD said unto me Behold, I have put my words in thy mouth.[54]

The Book of Isaiah allows us to establish the complete series in the play of equivalences. It contains, not in its first but in its sixth chapter, a vision similar to that of Ezekiel—Jewish prayer closely associates them—that ends as follows:

> Then said I, Woe *is* me! For I am undone; because I *am* a man of unclean lips, and I dwell in the midst of a people of unclean lips: for mine eyes have seen the King, the LORD of hosts./ Then flew one of the seraphims unto me, having a live coal in his hand, *which* he had taken with the tongs from off the altar: / And he laid *it* upon my mouth, and said, LO, this hath touched thy lips; and thine iniquity is taken away, and thy sin purged. / Also I heard the voice of the Lord, saying, Whom shall I send, and who will go for us? Then said I, Here *am* I; send me./ And he said, Go, and tell this people...[55]

For Isaiah too, the scorch mark on the lips opens up the path of a new word.

From the expression *eating the Book* we have thus taken up its second part: *Book ∼ fire*. The first, *eating*, in turn gives room to a play of fundamental equivalences.

---

[54] Book of Jeremiah, 1:6-7.
[55] Isaiah, 6:5-9

Chapter 4

As it is, Isaiah's narrative would suggest not only that the live coal replaces the signifier but also that incorporation can be replaced by contact of lips, the kiss—which explains to us the strange behavior of the faithful toward their religious books: they kiss them as they would a person they re-encounter or have to leave.

The equivalence *kissing* ∼ *eating* remains, however, oral. Another, more audacious equivalence, gradually comes into view: *eating* ∼ *reading*, clearly present in the custom of the first reading lesson, but also in the first text of Ezekiel mentioning in sequence *reading* and *eating*. Nor does our current language want for expressions in which eating and reading are given this equivalence. Finally let us examine the argument that we have been pretending to neglect up to now, that of sacrifices, the object of such an abundant analytical and ethnological literature.

A rite, as we have often enough repeated after Freud, over time evolves toward unveiling the desire it masks. In the Temple of Jerusalem, everything gravitated around the sacrifice whose symbolic structure we have been able to glimpse through the analysis of the *kashrut*. The worshiper making an offering would consume a part of the sacrificed beast, while the principal part would go to the priest.

Even before the destruction of the second Temple, the practice of sacrifice, at the instigation of the Pharisees, was relativized, precisely to the advantage of prayer or rather of reading: instead of performing a sacrifice and then eating the result, one would *read* the narrative of that sacrifice. Thus Jewish prayer took shape, to the rhythm of the ancient sacrifices—so well that the *Churban*, the Destruction of the Temple, really did not destroy the Judaism that was already functioning in other rites.

Jewish prayer really does not resemble a prayer at all. Only a small part is devoted to a codified and collective *asking* or *requesting* that God should watch over the needs of the people. It aims more at cementing group feeling than giving vent to the suffering of each of its members. The essential of this "prayer" consists of reading a sort of anthology of fundamental Biblical and Talmudic texts, gathered into a book, the *sidur*, a term that directly echoes the *seder*.

The holiday of Kippur, once so rich in sacrifices, comes to carry special significance for the substitution *reading* ∼ *eating*. Not only is it the moment of a strict fast but also the occasion for a continuous reading.

* * *

This set of facts sheds a peculiar light on the fundamental phenomenon of reading that our civilization seems so steadily to call into question.

It is imperative to point out at once that not all reading is equivalent. Certain reading belongs to relaxation, requiring only a bit of effort, other reading requires much more. Despite the great variety of possible kinds of reading, they seem to us to divide into two main categories.

There is "indifferent" or, shall we say, non-amorous reading. Here the reader invests in a text a faint curiosity that could either burgeon or end abruptly, in quest of information, or relaxation. So we read the newspaper or some currently "hot" book before tossing it away.

In total opposition to this is a second, "loving" form of reading—with its underside of hatred—that we prefer to call *canonic*. A certain number of books, among them the "sacred" texts, are the object of another sort of treatment. They are not suited to relaxation but rather to study, often requiring painful effort. One never tackles them without certain wariness, indeed without rituals, in a relation strongly tinged with anxiety. In the face of so many difficulties, the common run of mortals give up not on owning them but on reading them. They form the *skeleton* of any library worthy of the name. A minority, formerly the priests, manages to overcome these strange inhibitions; today their remote descendents do so through the transmission of the clerics, the intellectuals, organized into a subtle hierarchy.

Once the inhibition to read has been overcome, the effects of reading are often profound, leaving one feeling transformed in mind and spirit, joyful at times, although some ideal reader might find the particular reading of any given individual partial in the dual sense of fragmentary and obtuse. In short, canonical reading belongs to the very fringes of mystical experience, a communion.

Every human group—every people, every religion, but also every profession, indeed every association—possesses texts of this type, precisely called canonical, storing up the quintessence of the discourse that sustains it. Nowhere is this founding mechanism more clear than in Judaism.

The great reform of Judaism the prophet Ezra initiated was to make reading and study, here paired inseparably, as the *limud*, the

Chapter 4

cornerstone of the "invisible temple." *Limud* of what? Precisely of a *canon* of texts, the Jewish Bible or soon the Talmud, with which diligent, daily contact became the first commandment of the new Judaism. To shirk this contact more or less entails exclusion from the group—whence the palliative for ordinary mortals of the prayer already described. This *limud* took the place of the feasts and sacrificial roastings of the past.

I would relate the two modes of reading, as their names suggest, to the two of the forms of identification Freud described and which Lacan proposes connecting through the figure of the torus or ring. The "indifferent" reading (I), in a repetitive *demand*, it consists, like a spiral, in hugging the side hole of the toric air chamber. The "loving," canonical reading (II) encircles the central hole, supporting the function of desire.

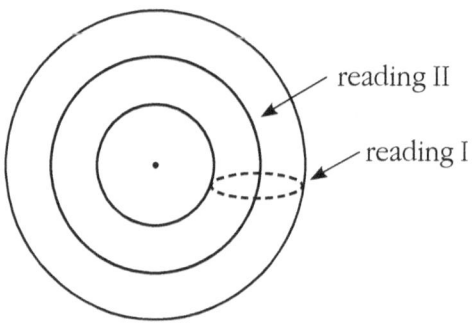

Figure no. 4
the two identifications and the two readings

From this point on we can set forth—while further demonstrating its more general application—our definitive conception of the group's founding primary identification.

Each group, we have said, is supported by a canonical *princeps* text, a statute, a *Brith* (covenant). The primary identification consists of maintaining with this text an intensive, almost devouring reading—a consuming that at privileged moments must be enacted literally.

Undoubtedly we have only established this mechanism within the particularity of Judaism, yet our last advances were already leading into its universality. The existence of canonical texts characterizing *every* human group does not seem a matter for serious dispute. The Bible and the Talmud of the Jews are immediately joined by the Christian Gospels and the Islamic Koran. No religion is without a similar body of texts. What do people do whenever they decide to intervene in the ideological domain in a new group? They draft a *manifesto* whose latent aspect is incorporation. Be it the humblest association—anglers, say—there is not a group that does not have its *statutes*.

This latency of real incorporation, of devouring, however, remains to be demonstrated.

It's not hard at all to show the *Book-eating* mechanism in Christianity. Certain readers might even accuse us of compounding the obstacles for developing our construction out of Jewish rites, when Christianity offers a much simpler and shorter path to establishing the same notion—thanks to the Eucharist.

Here I can't possibly enter into an adequately deep study of Christianity's most important rite. Suffice it to recall the main data most useful for our hypothesis.

The feeling of belonging to the Church comes, as we know, from the communion that consists of swallowing a consecrated wafer, the Host. Now, this wafer represents the body of Christ, that is to say, as Saint John teaches us, the incarnation of the Word: "And the Word was made flesh, and dwelt among us."[56] For our purposes, of course, the materialized signifier constitutes precisely the equivalent of writing at the moment it is eaten in the Mass.

The same John's Apocalypse, a text so important in the history of Christianity, develops the same principle at the same time that it forms a doublet, an attempt to conceptualize in Christian terms the fundamental Jewish text of Ezekiel's *ma'asei merkaba*. The Apocalypse likewise begins with a vision, rich in allegories, of multi-faced creatures. Then, with the opening of the seventh seal,[57] we read:

> And I saw another mighty angel come down from heaven .... And he had in his hand a little book open .... And the voice which I heard from heaven spoke unto me again, and said, GO *and* take the little book which is open in the hand of the angel which standeth upon the sea and upon the earth. / And I went unto the angel, and said unto him, Give me the little book. And he said unto me, Take *it*, and eat it up: and it shall make

---

[56] John, 1:14.
[57] Apocalypse [The Book of Revelations], 10.

Chapter 4

thy body bitter, but it shall be in thy mouth sweet as honey. / And I took the little book out of the angel's hand, and ate it up; and it was in my mouth sweet as honey: and as soon as I had eaten it, my belly was bitter./ And he said unto me, Thou must prophesy again before many peoples, and nations, and tongues, and kings.[58]

Could a comparative study of this text *almost* identical to that of Ezekiel swallowing the book epitomize, better than more extensive discussions, the divide that separated the Church from Judaism? It will suffice to point out the major variant. It has to do with the taste of the book: exclusively "*sweet* as honey" for Ezekiel, "*bitter* to your belly but in your mouth *sweet* as honey" for John. Does this absence of bitterness reflect the different position of Judaism in relation to the Book?

The fact remains, above all, that the operation of eating writing occurs in Christianity with incomparable straightforwardness and transparence, so great perhaps that it often passes unnoticed.

We needn't regret the efforts imposed by the choice of Judaism as terrain of study, of a phenomenon that presents, without the same clarity, a great wealth of ramifications, shifts, and equivalences that allow us, paradoxically, to better approach its universality.

Christianity's avowed ambition since its inception—to fulfill, down to the smallest detail, the letter of the word of the prophets, and thereby overcome, and open a way out of, the painful problematic of the father—is found again in its holy communion. What purpose, then, do these complicated dietary rites have, this regular, diligent reading of the Book? The result of the Eucharist was a kind of century-old long repression of the Book, a practice of the Index, consequently forming a symptom in which two terms are bound together: Book and Eucharist. Every modification of one deeply disturbs the other in the jolts that form the fabric of schisms and Christian heresies. Thus, to take only two episodes, the Lutheran Reformation, by reintroducing the Book, transformed communion; in our own times, the Vatican II council, acting in a similar direction, entailed modifying the Eucharist and certain fundamentalist backwaters.

[58] Ibid., 10: 1, 2, and 9-11

Christianity's schism with Judaism took the "circumcision of hearts" as a watchword. We find this too with regard to alimentary rites. Indisputably it produced a simplification, an effect of atrophying the structure, reduced now to this *imaginaire* of the heart. By an ironic role reversal, Judaism, in regard to the rite, proves to be more trinitarian than its offspring religion, maintaining its triple dimension: imaginary, to be sure, symbolic, (and how!); yet both are tied by the real of the act, the amputation of the fragment of prepuce flesh, or retaining the real Book and not the fragment of wafer one must eat.

I am convinced, without being able to show it precisely, that Islam too holds onto the same fundamental reference to devouring the Book. In fact the first lightning flash that prompted my construction was a chance encounter with traditional Islamic psychiatry.

From the depths of the African Sahel to the Muslim communities that have settled in Europe, *marabouts* (holy men) treat the mental illnesses of their co-religionists. One widespread practice consists in the therapist's writing down on a piece of paper a series of formulae, with the divine Name at the center. Then, as in the Jewish *sota*, this writing is placed in a vessel filled with water that the patient drinks.

In the hospitals of Paris, a study conducted with patients from the Magreb has taught us that they were familiar with this practice. It's impossible to believe there were not references to this in the canonical Islamic texts—though they remain to be found.

Step by step, then, we are verifying that *eating the Book* constitutes a universal operation, at least in the monotheistic world, derived from Judaism. To be sure, I have neglected the world of the Orient, and especially of China, knowing as little as I do about those cultures. However, a quick foray has shown me, in their wealth of dietary rites, various similarities with *kashrut*, for example, the need to remove some fraction of a given food.[59]

---

[59] *Li-Ji* or *Mémoires sur les bienséances et les cérémonies* [Memoirs Concerning Proprieties and Ceremonies], les Belles Lettres publishing society, Cathasia Sulliver, Paris, 1950. "One would not eat the tortoise that fed its little ones, nor wolf's intestines, nor dog's kidneys, nor filet of wild cat, nor the tips of a hare's back, nor a fox's head, nor the brain of a suckling pig, nor fish intestines, nor the tortoise's hind end."

Chapter 4

And it is almost unsettling to learn of the ideogram *shù*, denoting the book: a hand holding a stylet above ... a mouth.

The link of the Book to the oral object presents another manifestation that seems to warrant commentary beyond this brief remark.

Up to this point the incorporation of a single book seemed to create the sentiment uniting the group. Yet this object often divides, and radically so. Don't schisms, heresies, and conflicts originate from a different rereading of the same canonic text the right way? Everyone knows how violent the struggles of tendencies within a group can be: struggles that only amplify fraternal rivalry. This struggle—to which Saint Augustine bears witness in the famous first pages of his *Confessions*, where the view of the brother at the mother's breast brings a deathly pallor of jealousy to his face—derives principally from the oral object.

Judaism again proves exemplary here because it is not content to urge eating the Book; it surrounds it with commentaries, indicating in what ways the reading must be done, conjoining the written Law with the oral Law and with tradition.

After the effort to show directly, through numerous concrete examples, the existence of this primordial subjective activity of devouring writing, I hope I may at last be permitted to recall that current language bears an obvious trace of this phenomenon? Don't we know that gripping/exciting books are "devoured" while other less fascinating ones are "indigestible"? The examples of alimentary metaphors for books are legion in literature.[60] I'll content myself here with pointing out, since it is of such a different character, a scene in Selma Lagerlöf's *The Saga of Gösta Berling*, where the hero finds himself pursued by a pack of wolves.

> The wolves once frightened kept themselves at a distance. Yet soon, when the first amazement had passed, one of them shot out, with its mouth open and its tongue dangling out. Gösta quickly grabbed Mme de Staël's *Corinne* and hurled it at its jaws. This brought a moment of respite, while the beasts fought among themselves over this prey and tore it apart.[61]

---

[60] The French *Robert* dictionary provides an abundant collection. Those related to Rabelais strike us as especially valuable.

[61] Selma Lagerlöf, *Oeuvres I* (French translation) (Paris: Stock, 1976), 79.

Surely the wolf is the most eloquent symbol to denote hunger, and boundless hunger at that. The poet, as ever so clairvoyant in the realm of the unconscious, glimpses that the only object able to curb this hunger is the book. What Berling says in a few simple lines took me so many laborious pages!

CHAPTER 5

THE RAW, THE COOKED ... AND THE SYMBOLIC

The universality we have ascribed to devouring the Book meets with an important objection: the need for the Book, and thus of writing, which, though widespread, is not universal.

The origin of History is usually linked precisely to the appearance of writing. This empirical criterion proves, in passing, to have various structural reasons: if, for a subject, eating the Book takes on the history of his birth group, then writing and History clearly appear necessarily linked. Yet what was the status of that act before writing, how can one argue that man becomes man through eating the Book, when primitive peoples are characterized by their ignorance of it? In space as in time, two end-points seem to defeat our thesis.

With this impasse, the ethnology we've made fun of seems to have its revenge. Yet it will soon enable us to surmount this obstacle, and even give us greater precision in elaborating our argument.

A preliminary remark on the enigmatic relation numerous authors have pointed out between the signifier, the articulated sounds borne by a voice, and writing, allows us to narrow the gap between those peoples who have writing and those who don't. Here are two phenomena—speech and writing—of a totally heterogeneous nature, one preceding the other by several millennia. Yet when writing emerged, the signifier found in it a mold as though made to order, allowing it to be transcribed perfectly, without loss, as it were. The writing of the spoken word is not translation (which, as we know, is rife with impossibility and distortion), but rather, seems conceived to receive the Word within itself. This leads us to assume that *writing was always latent in language* and that its appearance was an explaining of existing relations rather than an emergence *ex nihilo*. Furthermore, no people, however primitive and prehistoric it may be, are totally without inscription.[62]

Nonetheless, this remark cannot erase the considerable phenomenon of the discovery of writing, or free us of the obligation to specifically examining primary identification among the people who lack writing, an examination we couldn't put off if by now we didn't have at our disposal the capital constituted by Claude Lévi-Strauss's magnum opus, *Mythologies*. In it, the author manages precisely to make his way into the edifice of myths through *The Origin of Table Manners*, the title of the third treatise. As a first step, let's content ourselves with examining the first of the four, *The Raw and the Cooked*. The inevitable choice required in approaching the myths of primitive cultures is that of orality, and Lévi-Strauss will on several occasions explain this necessity.

But before following the author in his dizzying exploration, allow me to comment briefly on his style and his method—both so elegant! *The Raw and the Cooked* opens with a long reflection on music, tasked with providing the Ariadne's thread of the mythological labyrinth. The structures of modern music, as Bach founded them in counterpoint and fugue, seem to him similar in form to the layered structure of myth. Beyond the analogy, Lévi-Strauss assumes that a filiation ties together music according to Bach and mythic knowledge. Through its disappearance in the West, an effect of the emergence of science, mythical thinking is thought to have engendered, through a mysterious transmutation, the art of counterpoint. Music was henceforth to be the magical route of access to the lost world of myth.

It strikes me, however, without underestimating the strange truth of this line of reasoning, that Lévi-Strauss finds his sturdiest supports elsewhere. First—as will surprise no one—in psychoanalysis. Structural anthropology was undoubtedly shaped more than by Saussurian linguistics, in the school of Freud's *Traumdeutung*: in telling a dream, to know enough to look past its apparent and often absurd signification in order to draw out of it the signifying elements, subject

---

[62] Lacan elaborated an important part of his seminar IX on *Identification* starting from the fact that prehistoric hunters marked each new prey they slayed by a line on an antelope rib. Similarly I would point out the enigmatic play of inscriptions found in the grotto of Lascaux.

The Raw, the Cooked ... And the Symbolic

them to certain transformative functions in order to extract the latent significations from them. The psychoanalyst who takes an interest in works in this genre is only reclaiming something of his own.

A second statement may seem more debatable, though it can be deduced from the earlier one: *the Lévi-Straussian analysis of myths is a child of Midrash*, not only because the filiation of psychoanalysis from it seems certain to anyone versed in these questions, but because it can be directly verified through Lévi-Strauss's own text. In particular we shall show the importance that *gezera chava*, or signifying transference, plays in it.

Experience shows us that a subject, in detaching himself from the culture he was born into, retains two cultural traits as final anchoring points, where, at times, surges of nostalgia are swallowed up: his group's culinary art and its music. Here Lévi-Strauss associates the two, profoundly. The Jewish people were never lulled except by one music and nourished on a single literature: Midrash. If the ethnological metaphor masked Freud's Judaism, did the musical metaphor play the same role in Lévi-Strauss?

For the fact remains that through him a new reflection on the question of rites, so essential in Judaism, is introduced into Western thought and subverts its prejudices.

> Rites appear as a 'para-language' that one can use in *two* ways. Simultaneously or alternatively, rites offer man the means either to modify a practical situation, or to designate and describe it. Most often the two functions overlap or translate two complementary aspects of a same process. But there where the empire of magical thought tends to grow dim and when the rites take on the character of a vestige, only the latter survives the former.[63]

Such an analysis may be directly applied to our own religions, so rich in alternations of mystical phases—where magical thinking is exalted—and ritualistic ones, where the "descriptive" aspect predominates. But then, what does the rite describe? Earlier we attempted to explain this: taken all together, the rites of a group sums up, in a "para-language" made of language, the history of this group, its body of myths. The rite becomes the memorandum and the reverse side of the

---

[63] C. Lévi-Strauss, *op. cit.*, 343.

myth, as Lévi-Strauss himself emphasizes, without going into detail. "This group... confirms whether there was any need for rite and myth to be in close connection."[64]

Anthropology would thus have to deal with a vast and unique field of study, the "rito-mythology," where mythology would form the place of the code.

But what have we to do with the myths? What can they teach us, who are subjects of science? "Indigenous philosophy," repeats Lévi-Strauss in several places, presents us with a vision of the world much closer to our own than we might have imagined.

Like all philosophy, it contains within it a *psychology*. To our surprise, this is revealed to be, at several points, close ... to Judaism, to certain conceptions that *kashrut* had taught. So Lévi-Strauss relates that the indigenous people classify beings according to the way they feed themselves, and separate the *civilized* eater of cooked meat, the carnivores who eat meat raw, the carrion eaters of corrupted flesh, the cannibals.[65]

Man may himself be identified with the animal in adopting the same eating behavior. A myth relates that a strayed hunter took refuge in a jaguar's den and was forced to eat like it. He steadily took on the jaguar's wild character and then its physical aspect. "From having eaten the jaguar's food, heterologous though it was to him, the man ends up identifying with the jaguar."[66]

The same theme is found in this other passage: "The Tarahumara is no longer like the coyote, which is content to tear a strip of flesh from a still quivering beast and eat it raw."

How intense would have been the great Kabbalist Benamozegh's joy, had he been able to read these lines: these primitive Tarahumaras respect the great Noachide principle *Evar min haḥaï*, that no man worthy of the name must ever eat a part torn from a living animal. Lévi-Strauss gives us to understand the import of this alimentary universal—to which we shall return.

The big concern, however, is not the psychology that might be expressed in the myths, but a *philosophy*, inseparable from an ethics, that is to say, of a particular economy of *jouissance*.

---

[64] *Ibid.*, 296.
[65] *Ibid.*, 292.
[66] *Ibid.*, 133-134.

This economy finds its ideal setting in *cuisine*.

Of all the codes that man can use to enunciate his messages, the alimentary code is certainly the most fundamental.... For man possesses five senses, the fundamental codes are five in number, thus showing that all the empirical possibilities are systematically inventoried and made to contribute.... [Yet] one of the codes occupies a privileged position: that which refers to the food regimens whose message the others translate, much more than it serves to translate theirs.... We begin to understand the truly essential place that accrues to cuisine in indigenous philosophy: it marks not only the passage from nature to culture; by it and through it, the human condition is defined with all its attributes, even those—such as mortality—which might seem the most indisputably natural.[67]

"Huxley suggested that the digestive process is comparable, on the mythic plane, to a work of culture.... There is certainly something true to this interpretation...."[68]

These conceptions, linking up with other concerns, prove close to ours, and one can imagine the comfort we felt in finding them at a moment in our reflection that seemed so rash.

Let us tighten this convergence even more. The object of anthropology is the study of this hiatus and at the same time this articulation, which separates nature and culture, a discontinuity that the phenomenon of religion covers up—whence this other Lévi-Straussian definition of anthropology as the science of the religious. Ever since *The Elementary Structures of Kinship*, Lévi-Strauss taught that the nature/culture opposition universally rests on the Law, that which prohibits incest. This same notion is designated in psychoanalysis as the *paternal function*, now specifically stating that it immediately takes hold of the tiny human being by the mouth, splitting the world into a cultural, humanized interior, and a natural exterior.

On this amply blazed trail, I want to establish a new equivalence with the devouring of the book—"eating, incorporating the myth"—thereby completing our construction.

The matter's not as paradoxical as it appears, since book and myth have more than one point in common. Myth, like the word in

[67] *Ibid.*, 172.
[68] *Ibid.*, 144.

Chapter 5

writing, demands only to merge into the book—as *Mythologies* attests—the myth is *read*, it possesses a "layered" structure, as Lévi-Strauss often and symptomatically repeats, designating a substantial reality beyond this wordplay.

"The layered structure of myth," he writes, "to which we have just been calling attention, allows us to see in it a matrix of significations set out in lines and in columns, yet no matter how we read, each plane invariably relates to another plane."[69]

These first arguments obviously have no demonstrative import and seek only to spark interest. Conviction, or at least the supposition of it, grows by sustained conversance with that masterpiece, *The Raw and the Cooked*, knowing that at one point a marked divergence will take place.

It opens, true to the musical metaphor, with the presentation of a theme, a founding myth (M1), reappearing throughout the book: *the bird nester (le dénicheur d'oiseaux)*.

This Bororo myth, which tells the epic of a heroic clan founder, begins with the incestuous rape of the mother. The father, having discovered the act, tries through a series of ordeals, to cause the death of his son, who, thanks to the complicity of his grandmother, eludes all the traps up until the crucial episode of the *bird nester* perched on the side of a rock. Once the son is in mid-air, the father removes the perch that had allowed the hero to hoist himself up to the nest, and abandons him in this unfortunate position. After various incidents, the young man gets through this last trial, finds the way back to the village, and avenges himself upon its inhabitants by a flood that puts out all the fires except the beneficent grandmother's.

Such is the starting point Lévi-Strauss chooses; out of it, by successive extensions, he embraces, in a truly grand unfolding, the essential of South American indigenous mythology, with ample incursions toward North America, then the rest of the world, to become, at last, truly cosmic.

Why should this humble little Bororo story warrant such honors?

If the goal of anthropology is to question the relation of culture and nature, and try to account for the manner in which the one emerged and detached itself from the other, this Bororo myth,

[69] *Ibid.*, 346.

according to Lévi-Strauss, would in its apparent fluidity contain a mythic response to this question, namely that *culture emerges with the discovery of fire*. The work contains many other examples of such myths, but that of the *bird nester* has the advantage of offering the most complete possible signifying chain. This thesis will be reasoned out, developed over the whole of the book ... and those that follow.

Myth of origin, then. No doubt every myth or legend, indeed every historical fact identified as such, invariably bears upon a point of origin, of a marked turning-point, for every "origin," even a partial one, of a phenomenon bears within it an enigmatic face, a hole in the chain of causalities and significations that the myth closes up. The hiatus filled in by myth Ml is considerable; it concerns the origin of origins, that primal repression coterminous with the emergence of man and which Lévi-Strauss suggests we should identify with the discovery of fire.

Let us be guided by this thesis for a moment. We should be immediately surprised by this interpretation of Ml as a myth of the origin of fire, because, in fact, the text of the myth makes only furtive mention of it, when it relates how a flood extinguishes all of the village fires.

The path by which Lévi-Strauss produces his demonstration is of great importance. It consists in paralleling the Bororo myth with a set of "variations" of Gé myths (M7 to M12) in which once more we find a *bird nester* in an unfortunate position, saved by the jaguar who teaches him the *use of fire*, until then unknown to men. The explicit connection here, *discovery of fire* ~ *bird nester*, by itself allows us, beyond the complex transformations Lévi-Strauss proposes, to suppose the same latent signification as in the Bororo myth M1.

We are quite familiar with this interpretative operation, our Midrashic *gezera chava* or signifying transference. First located in the overture of the work and at a decisive moment, it is not hard to find its trace in numerous other passages, revealing the unperceived debt of all structural thought to the Midrash.

The encounter with fire would thus indicate the appearance of culture, of man. Not fire as an abstract, archetypal element, in the manner of Jung or Bachelard, but concretely, as *cooking fire*. If cooking contains the code of a philosophy in which "the human condition is defined with all its attributes,"[70] then fire is its major signifier, the referent, the privileged cultural mediator.

This thesis—in the myths the primordial place reverts to the kitchen, to cuisine, and in this cuisine, to fire and the act of cooking—is recalled from one end of the book to the other:

> We are proposing to demonstrate [the first pages declare] that M1 (the myth of reference) belongs to a group of myths that explain the origin of the *cooking of foods*; that the site of cooking is conceived of by indigenous thought as a mediation ... that the myths view, in the culinary operation, activities that mediate between heaven and earth, life and death, nature and society.[71]

This project is echoed by these quotations taken from the end of the book:

> Where have we come to? ... Negatively and positively all the myths are related to the origin of food cooking. They oppose this way of eating to others, that of the carnivores, the carrion, etc.[72]

The cooked is related to the raw as culture is to nature.[73]

"Cooking" represents culture to such a degree that certain peoples "cook" all of a newborn to mark its becoming a human being:

> In Cambodia (as well, moreover, as in Malaysia, Siam and various regions of Indonesia) the mother, after delivery, stretches out on a bed or a raised grill beneath which a fire has slowly been burning. In America, the Pueblo mothers would deliver children on a pile of hot sand, the function of which was perhaps to transform the child into a 'cooked person' (as opposed to natural beings ... who are 'raw persons') ...
> Individuals intensely engaged in a physiological process are 'cooked': a newborn, a woman who has delivered a child, a girl in puberty. The conjunction of a member of the social group with nature must be mediated by the intervention of cooking fire which normally has the function

---

[70] C. Lévi-Strauss, *op. cit.*, 172.
[71] *Ibid.*, 72-73.
[72] *Ibid.*, 291.
[73] *Ibid.*, 342-343.

The Raw, the Cooked ... And the Symbolic

of bringing about the conjunction of the raw product and the human consumer, and thus through the operation by which a natural being is, at once cooked and socialized: 'Unlike the deer, the Tarahumara does not eat grass, but he interposes between the grass and his animal appetite a complicated cultural cycle ... and the Tarahumara is no longer like the coyote that contents itself with tearing a section of flesh off a still-living beast and eating it raw. Between the meat and the hunger he feels, the Tarahumara inserts the entire cultural system of cooking.[74]

This long quotation prompts the following remarks: the importance, first of all, in these questions of culture/nature, of phenomena that the author designates by the vague term of "physiological processes" and which concern the main moments of *the field of procreation*: menstrual cycle, birth—with the intimate link that this sexual domain has with that of death.

These moments, as our reading of *Totem and Taboo* has stressed, serve as privileged supports to the *rites*, among the primitives as well as in our cultures. The operation—metaphorical—of "cooking" is consequently only one particular rite in a vaster ensemble. The significance of those rites has been made clear: as nature seems to steal a lead over culture, the rite reestablishes the threatened equilibrium.

In keeping with magical thought, the cooking fire is not just a cultural mediator of the settlement; myth attributes to it a cosmic function.

Between the sun and humanity, the mediation of cooking fire is carried out in two ways. By its presence, the cooking fire avoids a total disjunction, it unites sun and earth and keeps man from the *rotted world* that would be his lot if the sun were truly to disappear, but this presence is also interposed, which is again to say that it fends off the risk of a total conjunction, which would result in a burned-up world.[75]

Whence the following meditation diagram:

---

[74] *Ibid.*, 342.
[75] *Ibid.*, 299-300.

Chapter 5

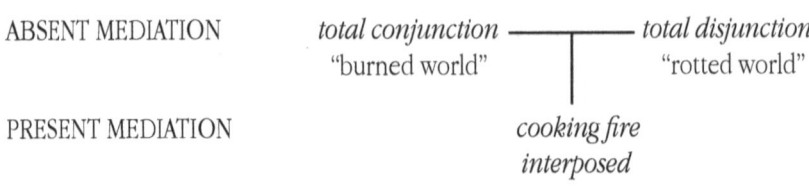

Figure no. 5

Isn't mediation culture itself? The diagram seems to carry a generality beyond the particularity—neither unique, nor perhaps the most important—of fire. It applies perfectly, for example, to another cultural operator, sacrifice—and allows us to grasp the universal scope that the Bible as well as the Tarahumaras attribute to the Noachide interdiction *Evar min habaï*.

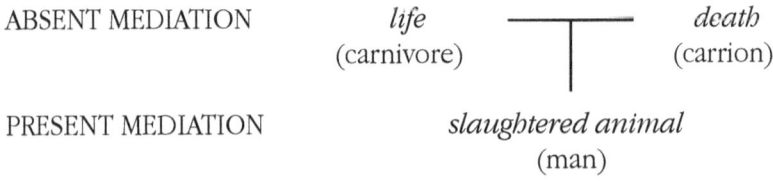

Figure no. 6

Lévi-Strauss does not neglect linking up his deciphering of myths with his earlier constructions, those of *The Elementary Structures of Kinship*, where the culture/nature opposition hinges on the prohibition of incest. Myth, for example, presents the excessive conjunction of sun and moon, i.e. of eclipse, as an equivalent of incest. The cooking fire concretizes this disjunctive mediation against the "burned world" of incest.[76]

The occasion thus arises to question a certain Lévi-Straussian ambiguity with respect to Freudianism. Everywhere, in fact, in his analysis of myths there spring up, to the point of diluting it, the notions that psychoanalysis has introduced into cultural commerce: the Oedipal theme, the devouring of the father, etc. Lévi-Strauss sails through

---

[76] C. Lévi-Strauss, *op. cit.*, 302.

them as if they were self-evident, without ever interrupting the flow of his own explanations, to underscore only the phenomenon he considers the ultimate one, the *discovery of fire*.

This mediating and conjunctive-disjunctive function of fire has a name in analytic theory: the *phallic function*. Which leads one to object to Lévi-Strauss's pyrocentrism: Can the discovery of fire be accepted as an ultimate referent of the passage from nature to culture? *Wouldn't such a conception be the "imaginarization," with Jungian echoes, of a more fundamental question?* Namely: *the enigmatic emergence of man, of culture, is signaled by the appearance of a first operator, the symbol, language, the signifier.* Fire only becomes a privileged mode for imagining that unthinkable thing: the role of the signifier for man.

Furthermore, fire and writing often seem to be two equivalent terms. The previous chapters allowed us explicitly to isolate this equivalence from the prophetic texts and from Midrash:

eating of writing = eating of fire

Chinese writing in its divinatory origins offers another eloquent example of the articulation *fire-writing*, because the first ideograms originated in the action of fire on bones or on tortoise shell.

What does it mean to cook, after all? To cook is to inject fire into a food and to transform that food by means of fire. All culture, be it Greek or Bororo, in characterizing man as an eater of cooked foods, presents him to us as an eater of fire; that is, if our equivalency *fire = writing* holds up, an eater of writing. Eating fire links all the operations of "cooking" evoked earlier—birth, puberty—the activity of the mouth, to a by now familiar signification: imprinting the cultural mark on a physiological activity, tying one to the other.

The strength of a great book—and *The Raw and the Cooked* is one—stems from offering the readers the material that allows a different interpretation than the one the text explicitly offers.

This other reading would thus consider the discovery of fire as a *second* moment, repeating and permitting the thought of a *first*, more fundamental, repressed moment: *the emergence of language*. Myth M10 clearly states:

Chapter 5

> In the past *men* did not know of fire and they would warm up their meat by exposing it to the sun on a flat rock so that it would not be completely raw.[77]

Here we are already dealing with a human society that discovers fire.

Lévi-Strauss seems strangely hesitant to broach the theme of the origin of language in mythic knowledge. He aptly cites a myth (M45) about this origin, where precisely the appearance of men and of language occur almost simultaneously; but no commentary, no transformation—so abundant at other, less important moments—accompanies it,[78] a silence no doubt correlative with certain of the author's theoretical and ideological *a priori*'s.

Yet the consequences of this silence seem decidedly minor. What is silenced at this precise point is proclaimed, repeated throughout the oeuvre. *The Raw and the Cooked* definitively reveals a split between a proscenium taken up by the thematic of fire and another scene, at least as important, where Lévi-Strauss presents his reflection in an entirely different light: precisely that of language. As soon as he states his thesis of fire-origin, he provides us with a second key:

> In the course of this book we shall establish that there exists an isomorphism between the opposition between nature and culture and that of continuous quantity and discrete quantity.[79]

This dimension of the discontinuous may not be the founding element of language, but it certainly is its necessary, imperative second condition: articulation. Underlying the foliated aspect of myth, it forms its mother lode, a genuine contrapuntal development—to keep within musical metaphorics—to the ensemble of significations exhumed throughout the book. Thus myths M2 and M3, telling how primitive humanity was decimated in crossing a river, elicit the following commentary:

---

[77] *Ibid.*, 79.
[78] *Ibid.*, 36.
[79] *Ibid.*, 60.

It seems, then, that the two myths, taken together, refer to three domains, each on its own originally continuous, but in which it is indispensable to introduce discontinuity in order to be able to conceptualize them. In each case, this discontinuity is obtained by radically eliminating certain fractions of the continuous. The continuous is impoverished and less numerous elements are now free to be deployed in the same space as long as the distance that separates them is enough now to keep them from encroaching upon each other or getting confused with one another.... Now, in any domain, it is only from the discrete quantity that one can construct a system of significations.

A diagram sums up this analysis:

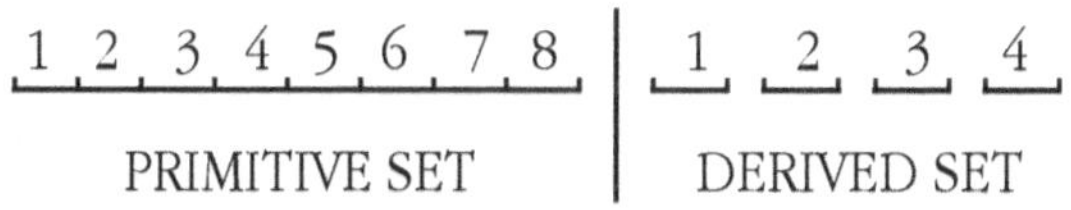

$$\underbrace{1\ 2\ 3\ 4\ 5\ 6\ 7\ 8} \qquad \underbrace{1\ \ 2\ \ 3\ \ 4}$$
$$\text{PRIMITIVE SET} \qquad \text{DERIVED SET}$$

Figure no. 7

I would gladly highlight every word of this remarkable analysis. No doubt because it echoes everything I've laboriously isolated in the analysis of Jewish *kashrut* and its redundancy, in fabricating, from a continuum, the discontinuous, which is synonymous with culture.

"The passage from nature to culture corresponds, in indigenous thought, to that from the continuous to the discontinuous," Lévi-Strauss will repeat further on. In indigenous thought? And so in ours! The very breadth of the intervals riddling the discontinuous has its function, identifiable precisely in the musical concepts of "diatonicism" for the large intervals and "chromaticism" for the small ones.

> Everything happens as if South American thought, resolutely pessimistic in its inspiration, diatonic in its orientation, *lent to chromaticism a kind of original wickedness*, so that the large intervals indispensable in culture, so that it may exist, and in nature, so that it may be conceivable, could result only from the self-destruction of a primitive continuum....[80]

The diatonicism/chromaticism criterion perhaps sheds a new light on various harped-on yet burning questions. The antipathy to-

---

[80] *Ibid.*, 286.

ward chromaticism is thus not peculiar to the South American Indians. Judaism, for instance, abhors it, and for each of its own rites shows the strongest predilection for diatonicism.

The cultural function of fire seems less and less the role of "head of the line" opposed to this second language-orientated analysis, of the phenomenon of culture: quite to the contrary, it is inscribed there and reinforces it in following the equation:

$$Continuous \longrightarrow discontinuous + remainder$$

because cooking has *diminution* as an immediate physical effect, deducting a fraction of the food by burning, transforming it into "perfume pleasing to God."

The Raw and the Cooked will thus conclude quite logically with considerations not about fire but rather about language.

> By taking its material from nature [we read on the last page], mythic thought proceeds like language, which chooses the phonemes among the natural sounds whose prattling provides it with a practically unlimited range.... For nature to lend itself to this role, one must first impoverish it: retaining from it only a small number of elements proper for expressing contrasts and forming pairs of oppositions.
>
> But, as in language, the rejected elements are nevertheless not abolished. They find shelter behind those promoted to the grade of leader.... In other words, the virtually unlimited totality of elements still remains available.... The plurality of levels therefore appears as the price paid by mythic thought for moving from the continuous to the discrete.[81]

Thus, from one end to the other, this simple operator, discontinuous/continuous, unfolds and manifests a prodigious explanatory potential.

Parallel to the myths of the origin of fire, Lévi-Strauss, at the start of the book, tackles another origin: *that of illnesses*. Bororo myth M5[82] relates that over the course of fishing, a woman, rather than transport the fish toward the village, greedily eats them all up until her belly swells, she vomits and thus exhales the first illnesses.

---

[81] *Ibid.*, 346-347.
[82] *Ibid.*, 68.

The origin of pathology and death is thus found to be related to *a woman* who can't manage to keep from eating and whose boundless gluttony brings on the ruin of the world. Under a different guise, we find again the theme of original sin, of Eve's wrong, eating what she was not supposed to. Morbidity, and thus the clinic, has its root in the "sin of the mouth," a wrong against culture, endangering humanization by a return to the state of nature, to the state of the continuous or unorganized, echoing what Freud called the *death drive*. We dig our tomb with our teeth, as the proverb has it.

Other myths confirm the oral etiology of illnesses, the pathogeny of the "wolf's hunger" that the father's moderating function doesn't temper:

> The parrot that says 'kra, kra, kra' is thought to be a human child transformed for having swallowed without chewing fruits roasting under ash and still burning. There too muteness is a result of incontinence.[83]

These observations, valuable for providing us with a better understanding of clinical phenomena, apparently lead to a negative conception of illness, an absolute evil. However, in one of those dialectical reversals that the author so artfully handles, the sick person is revealed as one of the figures of mediation precisely because he is *diminished*, in keeping with the equation:

$$discrete = continuous - remainder$$
$$(culture) \quad (nature)$$

In all these cases [we read], a discrete system results from a destruction of elements or from their removal from a primitive ensemble of which the author himself is a *diminution*.... The blind or lame, the one-eyed or one-armed are frequent mythological figures through the world, and figures that disturb us because their state appears to us as a deficiency. Yet just as a system made discrete by subtraction of elements becomes logically richer although it is numerically poorer, similarly the myths often confer on the disabled and the *sick* a positive signification: they incarnate modes of mediation.[84]

---

[83] *Ibid.*, 127.
[84] *Ibid.*, 62.

Chapter 5

The ill, the blind, the lame, Lévi-Strauss enriches the series with another figure, more startling:

> The *shut-in* who connotes a peculiar attitude toward the feminine world against which he refuses to distance himself, attempting, on the contrary, to take refuge in it.... The *shut-in*, the recluse, will be that person who, as we would say, 'clings to his mother's apron-strings.'[85]

These developments allows us to deepen the Freudian reflection on Judaism that we are engaged in, for the mediator figures that Lévi-Strauss comes up with are precisely those that Israel presents to the world—a source of violent ambivalences—through its founding patriarchs: Abraham, diminished by circumcision, Isaac, blind and groping about for the identity of his sons, and, above all, the last and leading patriarch, Jacob, who condenses in himself all the forms of mediation: "confined" with his mother, fond of cooking, and possessing the art of simmering the plates of lentils that will bring him the gold of paternal inheritance, to the detriment of his hyper-virile brother, the hunter Esau. Yet also, as a consequence of his wrestling with the Angel, from which comes the name Israel, Jacob is fundamentally the cripple, whose descendants preserve his memory—with a strange pride—in the prohibition against consuming the hind quarters of an animal. This same Jacob-Israel became known to men through that dream that is the most luminous example of mediation that has ever been invented: the ladder resting on the earth whose top is lost in the heavens.

The prophets, in turn—Moses and Jeremiah with their speech impediments, Job and his illness—will insist on this mediating function of the disabled man.

We understand better, beyond the secondary nationalistic overtones, this startling of the Jewish people to make themselves at once the "chosen people" and a "lame people." The awkward notion of chosen-ness fundamentally designates the function of mediation of Judaism between nature and culture, through rites that link it to the most primitive peoples and a Talmudic thought that places it on even footing with science, between East and West, between God and men.

---

[85] *Ibid.*, 65.

Let us add that the Jewish people collectively claim the place of "bride of God" and consequently a certain feminine position. The woman, indeed, since her anatomy incarnates castration, the supreme diminution, becomes the mediating figure par excellence among men, cultures, a privileged agent in divine action in History.

Evoking woman leads to the last and decisive objection in which the Lévi-Straussian and Freudian paths diverge. It has to do with the global lesson that Lévi-Strauss draws at the end of his book.

> And if one asks to what ultimate signified these significations refer that signify one another but which must in the final instance and all together relate to something, the only response this book suggests is that the myths signify the mind that elaborates them by means of the world of which it is a part....
>
> This is why it is vain to attempt to isolate privileged semantic levels in the myths: either the myths thus handled will be reduced to platitudes, or the level we assume to have crossed will give way, to automatically resume its place in a system always involving several levels.[86]

At the end of his trajectory, Lévi-Strauss encounters this entity hard to situate outside a theistic conception: the last "something" would be mind or spirit [*esprit*]. Against this *esprit* we will hold up that other conception to be culled from Freudian experience: why would the final term not be the *nothing*, a radical black hole in which the dizzying carousel of signifiers would be lost, and restart, a flaw in the structure that supports it, a hole of nonsense in the sense that proliferates?

Yet why should the *nothing* and Lévi-Straussian *esprit* be irreconcilable, and why shouldn't one be able to identify *esprit* with this hole that endlessly shifts, always elsewhere vis-à-vis the place one thought to seize and abolish it, and that creates eddies and vacuums on its edges? Because these two conceptions lead to this seemingly important divergence: absent if not downright "platitudes" for Lévi-Strauss, the "semantic levels" do exist for psychoanalysis: they appear on every page of the book without the ever-fluid text wanting to linger over them. The structural hole, the lack that characterizes the human phenomenon, is conjoined with what we have called the *field of procreation*, of sexuality and its impasses: the mystery of pregnancy

---

[86] C. Lévi-Strauss, *op. cit.*, 346-347.

Chapter 5

and of maternity, the enigmas of paternity and of filiation, and finally death, the inner lining of the whole of this field.

This Freudian position does not seem difficult to maintain through the very text of *The Raw and the Cooked*. From the first pages the connection between fire and the domain of procreation is established—though surreptitiously, as it were:

> A kraho myth, relating to a visit of a human hero to the house of the jaguar, contains the following remark that directly links the motif of fire with that of pregnancy: 'The jaguar's wife was very pregnant, on the eve of giving birth. Everything was ready for the delivery, above all a good fire flaming, because the jaguar is the master of fire.[87]

The conjunction, in the imaginary register, of maternity and fire finds its echo in the symbolic, in the opposition of the continuous to the discontinuous. Lévi-Strauss remarks that this synchronic distinction repeats the diachronic opposition of presence/absence, that same opposition which Freud, fundamentally, in the observation of the *fort/da*, connects to the mother.[88]

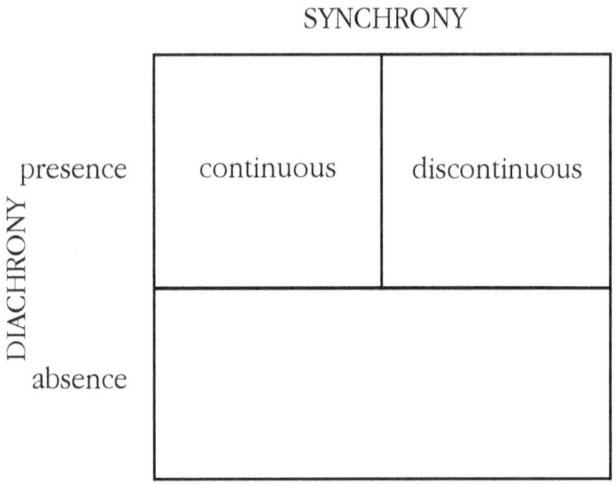

SYNCHRONY

	continuous	discontinuous
presence		
absence		

DIACHRONY

Figure no. 8[89]

[87] C. Lévi-Strauss, *op. cit.*, 80.
[88] S. Freud, Beyond the Pleasure Principle, in *S.E.*, vol. XVIII.
[89] C. Lévi-Strauss, *op. cit.*, 232.

The Raw, the Cooked ... And the Symbolic

These themes—maternity and paternity, birth and death, castration—chart an incessant saraband throughout the author's work, with special insistence in its middle, in the part entitled "Fugue of the Five Senses—The Opossum's Cantanta."

The question of the brevity of life and death is directly related here to food, and consequently to culture:

> The comparison between the apinayé and karaja versions of the origin of brief life offers another point of interest, namely that of making manifest the link between this motif and that of the origin of cooking. To light the fire, one must gather dead wood, thus credit the latter with a positive virtue although it is a privation of life ... between brief life and the obtaining of cooking fire, there exists an intrinsic bond.[90]

The function of femininity as privileged mediator, that through which knowledge comes to the world, but also birth and death—or, that which Eve's sin overlaps for us—is recalled, so to speak, in every myth.

> M77 ...: The first man, created by the demiurge, was living in innocence even though he possessed a penis always erect, which he would try in vain to make detumescent by soaking it in manioca soup. Through instruction from a water spirit ...the first woman taught the man how to soften his penis by engaging it in coitus. When the demiurge saw the flaccid penis, he grew angry and said: 'Now you will have a soft penis, you will make children, and then you will die; your child will grow up, he too will have a child, and will die in turn.'[91]

One could hardly express more clearly the dimension of Freudian castration. But, here as elsewhere, Lévi-Strauss, solely concerned with formal and structural considerations—important as they are—allows this text no further commentary.

With "The Opossum's Cantata," the enigma of the woman, mother and mediatrix, revives and expands.

Through a quotation of Florian, Lévi-Strauss at once presents this small marsupial as a "model mother."[92] The gé myths credit it with

[90] *Ibid.*, 159-160.
[91] *Ibid.*, 163.
[92] *Ibid.*, 172 ff.

Chapter 5

the origin of cultivated plants—mainly cereals—at the same time that they warn that eating this animal, the nurturing figure par excellence, brings on rapid aging and death.[93]

The natives likewise associate the emergence of this mythic figure with the differentiation of languages, peoples, and customs.

The opossum is sometimes substituted for the jaguar as a master of fire.[94]

The author extracts each of these significations, let us note, through an analogue process in the manner of Midrashic *gezera chava*, drawing parallels among myths of various origins.

Among these significations, let me point out one surprising attribute, of great importance, linked to the opossum, that of "stench," or "mustiness," associated in this context with maternity and with cereals.

This sundry constellation has already been encountered in the analysis of rites of the feast of Pesach: the emphatic, absolute prohibition of the *hametz*, a term that precisely designates the "fermented," the "corrupted." Our interpretation of the Jewish Paschal festival as one marking the separation of the subject from its mother, a preparation for the advent of this great saying that sums up the ten commandments: "I am he that led you out of the land of bondage" is reinforced here, and the meaning of *hametz* better situated in a coherent ensemble.

It seems legitimate in any case to assert, against Lévi-Strauss, that the dietary myths he analyzed indeed refer to a *privileged semantic level* that may well be impossible to designate by a particular signifier: the woman that man may be lacking, the field of procreation, the conjunction of sex and death, the phallic function, that of the Father—so many terms that are suitable without entirely satisfying.

* * *

The detour through anthropology allows us to give greater exactitude to that formula that is steadily becoming an algorithm: *eating the Book*.

---

[93] *Ibid.*, 172.
[94] *Ibid.*, 183.

The Raw, the Cooked ... And the Symbolic

The primitive, who not does dissociate his nourishment from the myths—which are the equivalent to the Book of our cultures and with which they certainly share properties—that underlie it, incorporates these myths in eating. The typical minimal figure of this incorporation is that of cooked meat: to eat cooked food is metonymically to swallow the fire injected by cooking into the food, a fire whose equivalence with writing has been established by numerous examples.

We find ourselves, in short, before a play of two-dimensional equivalences, representable by a system of Cartesian axes that would seem to define a *clinical space*. The terms indicated here are not exhaustive—others were noted earlier—but they do seem the pivot points of this space:

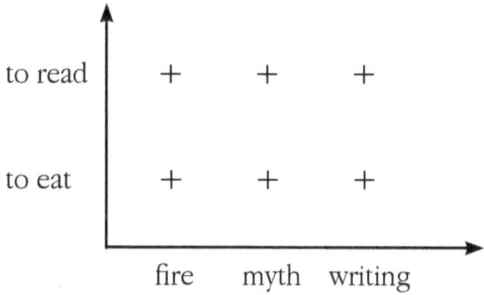

Figure no. 9

Our analysis might also be condensed in a table of coefficients whose combinations would provide certain clinical keys I will soon endeavor to explore.

	to eat	. . . .	to read	. . . .
fire				
mith				
writing				
. . . .				

Figure no. 10

CHAPTER 6

THE BOOK IN THE FREUDIAN FIELD

"What does a child in its mother's womb resemble? A folded book." — The Talmud

"Psychoanalysis teaches us that the child is father of the man." — J. Lacan

The human being eats writing to form, through the symbolic, his psychic reality. Is this thesis as atypical as it seems within the corpus of psychoanalytical theory?
Its best-established anchoring point is the concept of the oral drive and its primordial function in psychic organization. But that concept on its own, as we usually understand it, doesn't justify my construction, which summons it up only in light of a knowledge of dietary rites and myths.
We find traces of oral concerns from the very dawn of Freud's writings, precisely associated with Jewish dietary rites and their implicit reference to original sin. Thus, in this letter to his fiancée, oft-quoted, since his Jewish heritage so interests the Freudologues, we find these arguments from of an old Jewish printer and publisher, to which Freud quite clearly adheres:

> Let us take, for example, the dietary rites, what can be more indifferent than what one eats? ... Let us go back to the story of the Creation. It may be a fable, but a thing in which humans have believed for ages cannot be absurd and must have some sense. When God had created the first men and placed them in the Garden of Eden, wasn't the first commandment that he gave them a commandment concerning food? Why was it not a moral commandment?[95]

---

[95] S. Freud, *Correspondance*, 1873-1939, letter 7, July, 23, 1882, in *Letters of Sigmund Freud, 1973-1939*, ed. Ernst L. Freud. (London: Hogarth Press, 1961).

Chapter 6

The theme of "eating the Book" becomes almost manifest in a dream considered crucial to Freud's "autobiography," the *dream of the botanical monograph*.[96]

This dream allows him to recover a childhood memory of great importance: his father had let him *pull* a voluminous illustrated book to pieces, its leaves plucked "like an artichoke," as he puts it—a highly eatable object. Freud relates two elements from his adult life to this scene. On the one hand, the choice of the artichoke as a preferred flower or vegetable, and at the same time his boundless taste for books, his excessive purchases in the bookstore, which had encumbered him with debts. Finishing this analytic fragment with a word, Freud terms himself a *Bücherwurm*, "a bookworm," one of those worms that eat away at books and indeed live off them. By now, of course, we must admit that we're all *Bücherwürmer*.

From what hefty illustrated book might Freud have inherited his passion at once for books and for artichokes—a highly "layered" vegetable? If Freud's text does not indicate it, Théo Pfrimmer's book raises the hypothesis that the volume in question was the family Bible, the Bible illustrated by Philippson, into which Freud, by his own admission, plunged very precociously, before he could even read.[97]

This theme later seems to disappear from Freud's writings. Yet a careful reading allows us to make out its continued presence.

The first example comes up in his first case history, the analysis of Dora.[98] This young hysteric has obligingly joined in a quadrille in which a couple of friends, the K.s, stand in for the parental couple. Mrs. K. is Dora's father's mistress, while the husband has been trying to seduce Dora. To these five characters of tragi-comedy who've made so much psychoanalytic ink flow, we must add—as few authors have seen—an object: a voluminous dictionary which, like a ferret, pops out or can be imagined as present when one least expects it. Thus, in that crucial moment said to belong to the second dream, Dora dreams that she is reading a letter from her mother informing her of her father's death.

---

[96] S. Freud, *The Interpretation of Dreams*, in *S.E.* vols. IV and V.
[97] T. Pfrimmer, *Freud lecteur de la Bible*, (Paris: P.U.F, 1982).
[98] S. Freud, Fragment of an Analysis of a Case of Hysteria [Dora], ch. 3, in *S.E.*, vol. VII.

We know, since Freud stressed the point so heavily, that the death of the father, for every man, is the most tragic event of his existence. It is all the more so for a hysteric, whose whole structure is dominated by love for the father. How does Dora react to this death? First by forgetting its aftermath in the dream: "The forgotten and later remembered parts of a dream," writes Freud, "are always the most important for understanding." Then this forgetting is dispelled and Dora recalled that, "she went calmly to her room, and began reading a big book that lay on her writing-table."

Freud questions her: "I asked whether the book was in encyclopedia *format* (*Lexikonformat*), and she said it was." He concludes laconically, but surely too quickly: "If her father was dead she could read or love as she pleased." Dora did indeed draw all her sexual knowledge from the *avid* reading of this lexicon, knowledge that forms the framework for her psychic reality.

Thus Dora readily consoles herself for the death of the dearest person of all with a dictionary, which appears to perfectly replace the Dead Father.

The book that comes up in Dora's case may be found in many treatments of hysterics, and first of all in the most famous of them all, because it was the first one in the history of psychoanalysis, that of the hysteric known as Anna O. Here too, we find a book casting a large shadow—in this case a collection of Shakespeare's works—which stuck so firmly to the tongue and palate of this young German-speaking Jewess that during her illness she could speak only English—hence the coinage of such famous expressions in psychoanalysis as "chimney-sweeping" and "talking-cure." This symptom, unique in the annals of psychoanalysis, has never been interpreted despite the abundant literature Anna O.'s case has prompted. Might she not have "swallowed" Shakespeare as a replacement for her own dying father?

The relation of Dora to the lexicon leads to other considerations. If the canonical Book, of religious origin, constitutes the cornerstone of psychic reality, for Dora this place is allotted to the dictionary. Let's not hesitate to generalize: this type of book replaces scripture for mankind in the scientific era, for the subject of science whose attachment to revelatory religions has come undone—the attachment, say, of a pious Jew to the Book, the Torah. Man in our scientific era awaits his "revelations," or gets his references, only from some decent dictionary.

Chapter 6

Dominique, a woman patient, tells me in one of the first sessions of her treatment: "I've decided to return to reality: I've opened my dictionary." This has become our field of reference, the book of books, "reality." If a Frenchman wants to check his knowledge on any question whatsoever—scientific, literary, geographical, etc.—he opens the *Littré*. The pious Jew acts in the same way, only he opens not a dictionary but a Bible or a Talmud.

Let me also point out the following metamorphosis of customs. In the past, when a child learned to read, people solemnly offered it a Bible. Today, as the scholar G[eorges] Duhamel counsels, "The finest present one can give a child once it knows how to read is a dictionary." Likewise, it used to be said of an erudite man: "He's a *Sefer Torah*, a Bible." Today we prefer to call him a "dictionary" or a "walking encyclopedia." The very form of the dictionary, down to its paper, imitates the Book, making it the sacred book of laymen.

To verify this equivalency of Bible ~ dictionary, just open to the entry "dictionary" in a dictionary.[99] You'll find that the very notion of such books is recent, contemporary with the emergence of science. It's true that the Latins inaugurated such an enterprise in the 2nd century C.E. with the *Onomasticon*, but the real venture begins in the 16th and 17th centuries.

A number of authors have underscored the equivalency pointed out here. Anatole France, for example, wrote, "To be fair, the dictionary is the book par excellence. All other books are contained within it: it is only a matter of extracting them from it. What, after all, was the first occupation of Adam when he left God's hands? Genesis tells us he first named the animals by their name. Before anything else, he made a dictionary of natural history." Baudel, above all, had the following intuition: "I see in the Bible a prophet whom God orders to eat a book. I do not know in what world Victor Hugo first ate the dictionary of the tongue he was called upon to speak."

* * *

---

[99] In this instance, I have chosen the 11-volume *Robert*.

Another presence of the Book in Freud, more subtle, no doubt, which opens up important perspectives, may be found in his *General Introduction to Psychoanalysis*, specifically in the crucial chapter on transference.[100] Everyone knows, of course, that Freud was especially fond of botany and had a solid knowledge of it. "Transference," he writes, "may be compared to the intermediary layer between the tree and the bark, a layer that provides the starting-point for the formation of new tissues and the augmentation of the trunk's thickness."

This same metaphor, "between tree and trunk," is likewise found elsewhere to designate the unconscious itself, in Freud as in Lacan.

Now, as it happens, in botany, this "between bark and tree" is called *liber*, the etymology precisely for the Latin *liber*, "book," and French *livre*, since the first medium for writing was this intermediary layer easily detachable in certain species.

Implicitly, then, Freud offers us a theory of the transference structured like a book.

The term *liber* is revealed, moreover, to be a nodal point teeming with significations, spread over two opposite sides a hair-breadth's apart.

The same *liber* is, in fact, at the root of the word "liberty." That the book and the thwarting of tyranny should plunge their roots in at the same point is certainly richly instructive. The allegory of Ezekiel eating the Book depicts for us—a point we must come back to—a process of emancipation.

We also find book-liberty in the signifier "delivery" designating the end of the labor of childbirth. Our language thus recovers the Talmudic equivalency between child and book, which is surely universal.

Liber, moreover, also refers to another side, *that of alcohol and of mythology*. *Liber* or *Liber Pater* is, in fact, the Latin name for Dionysus, Bacchus, from whom we derive the term "libation." It comes from the translation of Laius, the "Liberator," an epithet given to Dionysus, liberty being understood here as outside the law.[101]

---

[100] S. Freud, *A General Introduction to Psychoanalysis*, lecture 27, in *S.E.*, vol. XVI. I am extracting what follows, almost in the raw state, of the discourse of a woman patient, M., suffering from an ethylism from which she recovered. Unaware of the concerns I am presenting here, she managed to decipher this on her own.

[101] Since in these pages we are consulting the dictionary, it is the *Grand Larousse encyclopédique* that provides us with these details. Article *Dionysos*.

Chapter 6

A short detour through mythology informs us that this god was procreated following an unusual scenario. His mother, Semele, dies in the sixth month of gestation, and Zeus, the father, will carry the fetus sewn into his thigh. As in the couvade, and as in every assumption of paternity, the father occupies transitorily, imaginarily, a feminine position. Yet incontestably the myth of Bacchus-Dionysus pushes this particular to its extreme, representing *a deeply disturbed mode of paternity*.

This disorder unfolds and expands in the cult devoted to this god, in the cruel orgies called *bacchanals*.

Dionysus incarnates the subjective position of refusing the law of the city by living at its margin, in contact with it, but in refusal.

> Dionysus never entirely enters into the city. His temples there are rare, he is more often outside of the city than in it. A whole aspect mentioned about him emphasizes this refusal of the political and of socialized life.

The subject does not completely cross the gap that divides nature and culture, he demands proximity, attachment to Mother Nature. Curiously, this position is translated into behavior and rites related to food:

> Sharing is carried out in culinary terms: the city encourages eating the cooked flesh of domestic animals sacrificed according to the rules that designate what portion is reserved for the gods and what portion accrues to men. In Dionysism the model is omophagia: to eat raw the flesh of an animal victim captured and torn apart at the end of a wild pursuit.

What do we find there, but once again the Noachide law *Evar min haha*ï, to eat only sacrificed meat, so trivial at first but which progressively confirms its essential cultural function, which *kashrut* consolidates. The Bacchic cult consists first of calling into question, denying, this universal dietary rite. Tearing apart prey in the manner of a carnivore is called *taref* in Hebrew, which is to say, the opposite of kosher.

Also reappearing in all dietary rites is the permanence of a *remainder* that returns to God in order to institute the discontinuity necessary to the symbolic, it too a function denied in Dionysism.

Thus one departs (our author concludes) from the system that founds the human condition in a dual relation: with the gods and with men. Dionysus draws his faithful into a nature external to the city, where beasts, men and gods are merged and interchangeable.

To lead them where? No doubt, into extreme barbarism:

The Bacchants behave like ferocious beasts and Agave brings the head of her son hunted down by the pack of women whom she leads. At the extreme, Dionysus compels anthropophagy. One tips here into a time before society, in which men eat one another like savage beasts.... The plane of bestiality is confused with the golden age. Dionysus ushers in the reign of Unity, prior to the time of difference.... [He] erases the traumatizing division between gods and men.

Only, by suppressing the Law which they do not ignore and yet deny, Bacchus and his remote disciples introduce an even greater trauma: barbarism.

Dionysus is one figure among others of these cruel religious deliriums around maternal divinities in the time before Mount Moriah, where the arm of Abraham is halted before striking the neck of his son. Agave, like all the Canaanite *baalim*, in killing her son, scoffs at the interdiction of the Father who tells her, "Thou shalt not re-incorporate thy offspring." This theme of the Mother and of the return to her, to nature, to the golden age, to which the Father objects, is at the root of all individual pathology as well as of the great barbarous collective deliriums of every age, our own in particular.

The incorporation of the Book, that stick thrust into the jaws of the crocodile to prevent their closing over their prey, the subject, seems here in part failed, not entirely absent but unstable, unaccomplished. The drama of every alcoholic, as we shall soon see in detail, plays out against this background: a troubled, indeed impossible, paternity.

* * *

Let us point out a final reference, furtive but very valuable, in Freud's text, if not to the Book, to writing. It occurs in the twilight of his oeuvre, in the famous *Civilization and Its Discontents*:

Chapter 6

Writing was in its origin the voice of the absent person; and the dwelling-house was a substitute for the mother's womb, the first lodging, for which in all likelihood man still longs....[102]

The sentence is ambiguous. Is it asserting the equivalence of writing and the maternal body? The old Midrashic principle of contiguity of statements that Freud adopted allows us to say as much. And is there, after all, anyone more radically absent than the mother?

An author of utmost importance, Melanie Klein, removes any last doubts on this score: writing is indeed the equivalent of the mother's body. She says so in various texts, but especially in her book *The Psychoanalysis of Children*. She is also familiar with the link between reading and childbirth.

"Reading, too," she writes, "in consequence of the symbolic equation of her mother's body with books, had come to mean a violent removal of substances, children, etc. from the inside of the mother."[103]

From a starting point and in a formulation quite remote from mine, Klein thus comes to convergent conclusions—with one important exception: the Book is a maternal symbol, whereas in my view up to now it's been linked to the father.

Before commenting on this divergence, let us examine a text by another eminent student of Freud's, influenced in this context by Melanie Klein, James Strachey, the author of the canonic *Standard Edition* who—should it surprise us?—devoted an article to "Some Unconscious Factors in Reading.[104]"

Articulated into the category of drives—which Freud, in a veiled criticism of certain of his students' production, called "our mythology"—this short text offers numerous unexpected similarities with the theses of this book.

One finds in it above all the plain statement that reading, even if it calls into play other mechanisms, is the substitute for eating, the sublimation of orality, a thesis supported by the clinical observation of reading difficulties but also by language observations. Like French,

---

[102] S. Freud, *Civilization and Its Discontents*, in *S.E.*, vol. XXI, 91.
[103] M. Klein, *The Psychoanalysis of Children*, trans. Alix Strachey (London: Hogarth Press, 1949), 93. Also cf. 199 and 282.
[104] In *International Journal of Psycho-Analysis*, 1930, vol. XI.

English presents numerous alimentary metaphors for reading: a voracious, omnivorous reader, etc.

Strachey, in passing, addresses the two modes of reading we earlier identified as "indifferent" and "canonic" readings, which he himself terms "easy reading" and "problematic reading." For him, the reason for this split has to do with the division of the oral phase into two moments: a moment of liquid then of solid nourishment, or sadistic-oral. This genetic explanation, interesting as it is, obviously doesn't take into account the essential of the phenomenon.

Quoting Klein, but also Freud and Glover, he takes up the equation:

Book = mother's body devoured in reading

Yet the forced, strongly regimented character of the operation inevitably evokes a paternal participation that Strachey reintroduces by making reading an equivalent of ... coprophagy,[105] a perversion that the Kleinians interpret as a symbol of the incorporated paternal penis. Reading, through this acrobatic deduction, becomes a devouring of the father.

Strachey, finally, doesn't neglect to mention Ezekiel.

The equivocation remains: Is the Book a paternal or maternal equivalent? Without a doubt, there is a feminine component to the Book when one considers the tenderness a devout Jew manifests when he carries a Torah scroll in his arms or when he wraps it up again in its finery. Such gestures of piety also suggest the care lavished on a baby.

But the Book's *father*-component seems to me the prevalent one. Lacan's theory of paternal function, of structural and linguistic inspiration, allows us to simply resolve this vacillation. To speak of a maternal "substitute" or "equivalent" clearly indicates the subject's insertion in the symbolism of language. How else, indeed, can the pages of a book replace the mother's body? There is a substitution of signifiers. That of the Book—and of the love one bears to it as towards the father—overlaying the desire of the mother. This substitution—or rather

---

[105] The theme of coprophagy, appears, moreover, in Ezekiel.

Chapter 6

this *metaphor*—is the same one that defines the father as a regulatory point for the whole structure of language.

Furthermore, for ages, the Kabbalists sensed and commented at length on the feminine and maternal dimension that looms behind the austere figure of the Father.

Thus, Melanie Klein and above all Strachey, by their own different paths, reached elements of conclusions very close to those of the present text. Yet they didn't dare to take the decisive step and grasp that this operation of eating the Book was the truth of Freud's vagaries—and intuitions—relating to the totemic meal. Had they done so, they would have ironed out a fair number of difficulties concerning primary identification and the superego.

With Lacan, the nodal point of the incorporation of the Book is thoroughly clarified. His reflection on the Freudian superego already set him on the right track. How, he asks, could Freud invent this agency made of language, by giving it orality as a root, except by introducing the hypothesis, crazy though it may seem, of a human being who eats words?[106]

Some years later he concluded one of the strongest moments in his teaching, his seminar on *The Ethics of Psychoanalysis*, with a beautiful, long meditation on Saint John eating the Book.[107]

This time, rather than the superego, it is another aporia of Freud's that Lacan wants to illustrate: that of sublimation, in which the drive is satisfied without repression but by changing its aim. What better example to take than that of orality, seemingly so close to biological needs?

"There is eating," he says. "Of what? The Book, [which in] this powerful image becomes the incorporation of the signifier itself."

This operation, he continues, "occurs every day." But sublimation is necessarily paid for by a renunciation of *jouissance*, by a "pound of flesh" (*livre de chair*) whose recovery is precisely the function of religion—the pound of flesh whose fall we have, at every stage, verified as punctuating the stages of the *kashrut* or the examination of dietary

---

[106] J. Lacan, *Le Séminaire, livre IV: La Relation d'objet*, (Paris: Éditions du Seuil, 1994).

[107] It escaped him, no doubt, that Ezekiel had used the same metaphor before the *Apocalypse* of John.

myths, creating the discontinuous and the symbolic. Thus enters the concept of *desire*, which this loss stirs up.

Where does this blind human desire lead, having taken refuge today, according to Lacan, in the man of science?

> The future will reveal it to us, perhaps on the side of those who by the grace of God have most recently eaten the Book, those who have not hesitated to have written it, this book of Western science, with their efforts, indeed with their blood. It is no less an edible book.... The important thing is not to know whether man is originally good or bad, the important thing is to know what the Book will provide when it has been completely eaten up.[108]

In the enigma of desire, in its metabolism, the Book plays its unnoticed role.[109]

However, not even Lacan draws all the consequences of the mechanism he brings to light, the answer it contains to the difficult question of primary identification. No doubt this was because the reality of the incorporation of writing eluded him, this reality that we have discovered in the *seder* of Rosh Hashanah.

* * *

Where does all this lead? Inevitably, straight toward the clinic, the most directly observable and most classic place.

We haven't, in fact, ceased asking the fundamental question of psychoanalysis, the one that supports its edifice: the paternal function, that strange chicanery by which, passing through castration, the subject himself accedes to desire and paternity. A crucial moment that mobilizes the whole of the structure, with acceptance of this fact that doubles with or differently expresses sexuality: death. A chicanery rich in equivalences, for which Freud drew the equation:

---

[108] J. Lacan, *Le Séminaire*, livre VII: *L'Éthique de la psychoanalyse*, (Paris: Éditions du Seuil, 1986) / The Seminar, Book VII: *The Ethics of Psychoanalysis*, trans. Dennis Porter. (New York: W.W. Norton, 1997).

[109] Clinical observation easily verifies this role. An obsessional woman patient, for instance, declared that at the start of her puberty, "Books suddenly replaced dolls," those ersatz objects of her childhood desire.

Chapter 6

feces ~ penis ~ child

enriched first by a term, that of the *Book*, then by two other terms, provided by the study of myths: *fire* and *myth* itself, ancestor of the Book. Thus we get this new, enhanced chain:

feces ~ penis ~ fire ~ myth ~ Book ~ child
⎯⎯⎯⎯⎯⎯⎯⎯⎯⎯⎯⎯⎯⎯⎯⎯⎯⎯⎯⎯⎯⟶

Concerning this child, marvelous as it must be, is it not said that with its appearance the family circle widens, that is to say, that it accepts the newcomer? The operation has its difficulty if we think of the sibling jealousies or that at this precise moment the parent's psychosis may burst out. Yet most often the "happy event" is well and quickly integrated into the family set-up.

One thinks less of the inverse operation, far thornier, the one by which the new subject must recognize this group into which he is born, this people of which he is a member despite himself, filled with an always painful history, rich perhaps in some facts of glory but also of any number of dramas and humiliations, harrowing episodes, aspects of cowardice or feebleness, and internecine rivalries. The newborn must drink this bitter chalice of family history perpetuated in its present structure in order to take his place in the succession of generations. Such is the principal signification that I attribute to the devouring of the Book: to accept his inscription in the history of the group, his place in the procession of its generations, and now bear in himself the promise, the potentiality of the future procreative act. What does the Book in man's belly resemble? To paraphrase: the promise of a child to come inscribed into a lineage.

This question of desire, the far end of psychoanalytic questioning, summons for evidence its origin, its mysterious cause. Freud grasps its outlines:[110] a disappointed *jouissance*, a "*manque-à-jouir*" (a "lacking-*jouissance*") with which all experience seems stricken, compared to a mythic first *jouissance*.[111] The same text of Freud teaches us that this worn or dented human *jouissance* is narrowly associat-

---

[110] S. Freud, *Project for a Scientific Psychology*, (1950 [1895]) in *S.E.*, vol. I.
[111] We know the breadth that Lacan will give to this perspective with his *objet "a."*

ed—being, in fact, its effect—with a certain knowledge, structured like all human knowledge, following the laws of language. The lost part of *jouissance*, incommensurable, is thus at one with a gap, a lack in knowing that makes all *absolute knowledge* forever impossible.

Psychoanalysis found its birthplace in this fault, this rift, that Freud called "primary repression," part of knowledge about the origin, at once inaccessible and structuring psychic reality. The power of religions over man has to do with their claim to be in possession of this last secret.

A pressing need for a subject to accept this limit to knowledge that amputates it, is that there are things that cannot be spoken nor judged. The illusion of a possible absolute knowledge leads to wild, endless imaginings, to pathology, to delirium. Mystical effusion, outside the symbolic, is in vein.

Eating the Book is only a fresh formula to designate the forming of that original repression. Umberto Eco's novel *The Name of the Rose* nicely illustrates this mechanism. A medieval monk considers it necessary for the well-being of the world that a work of Aristotle's on laughter, of which he possesses the sole copy, should remain unread. He poisons its pages so that any bold reader's contact ends in his death. Then, as no maneuver he can devise manages to deflect human curiosity, he will end up literally eating the book and dying of it; Aristotle's knowledge about laughter thus becomes part of inaccessible knowledge.

This amputation of the symbolic, as painful as it seems, is nevertheless the condition for the system not to be closed and deathly, so that a certain play, a share of ambiguity, may remain possible in language with its heaping up of metaphors and its whirl of metonymies through which human desire may slip. The subject can then, like the prophet, answer the summons: "Go forth and speak!"

In opposition to this, every totalitarian project rests on the illusion of a possible absolute knowledge.

Experience shows how difficult this assumption is, leaving room for a rejection without appeal for anyone who opens the doors of a psychosis. By a sad return of the real, for want of having been eaten, the Book will eat the person who has failed in his task.

Most often, the person who has incorporated the Book will repress the indissoluble pact through amnesia. This position immediately entails a structural regression. Along what line of defense? Our chain of equivalences shows it: on the line of myth, on that "individual myth of the neurotic" that Freud discovered quite early on. The subject invents for himself another family history made of wealthy or heroic princes. Such a myth accompanies and masks a violent hatred of his real family, his cultural and religious group, then following the boomerang course of every drive against the only object truly within his scope, the one who suffers the greates destruction in the operation: himself.

This neurotic amnesia may, when exacerbated, leave room for the denial of the operation itself. The bolstering of the mythological current may become mythomania, indeed a more severe regression on that earlier theme—fire. At that point, clinically the oral perversions are established, the most widespread of which is alcoholism.

* * *

An important objection comes to mind. I've described a quite complex mechanism here. How does the little human being, so helpless, come to find his way, accomplish operations so paradoxical, identify himself, repress, incorporate, etc.?

Here we should not repeat the curious silence of *Totem and Taboo* about the *true operator* of this set of processes: the mother.

Maternity presents the enigma, nearly unthinkable for the masculine mind, of a love so pure that it accepts the quite uncommon renunciation of *jouissance*—which a mother could draw from her little one and which the latter demands of her—so that the function of desire may come to it. The newborn, in its overall prematurity, tends toward one goal alone: to form a perfect dyad with its genetrix, to be her exclusive pole of interest. Just her absence is enough for the nursling to live that instant as an antechamber of death.

Now, this same newborn must soon discover that its mother, whatever her devotion is like, seems attracted by a second pole that excludes it, a pole veiled to it, enigmatic, the phallus, whose bearer is the father. The dyad of its wishes runs aground into a triad. In the forced questioning of what "makes her run," the child encounters the Book that the mother, veiled in the paternal metaphor, places within its grasp. The child eats it in the weaning from the breast, thus identifying with his father and with the order of generations that he introduces.

Here, then, are the significations and the numerous, varied effects for this incorporation of the Book. They are not independent, and form a network, facets of a complex phenomenon whose interconnection isn't easy—though it is desirable—to identify. *Figure 11* serves essentially as a reminder and summary of this.

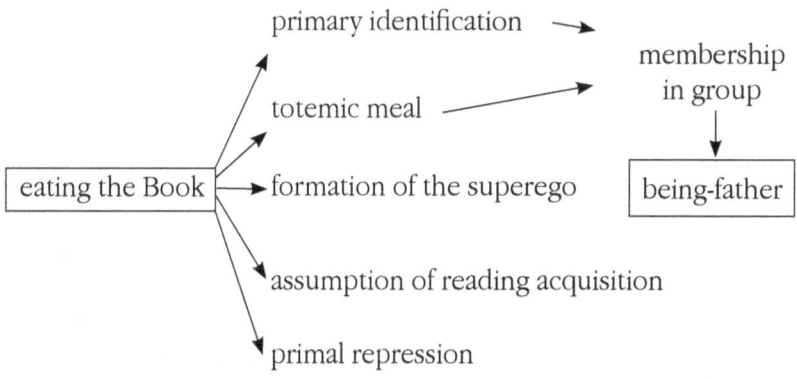

Figure no. 11

Let me add, finally, that the eating of the signifier is not specific to man, that the animals Lacan punningly calls "*d'hommestiques*" also participate in it. Pavlov's famous experiment attests to this. What, after all, is that poor dog put through? A food is associated with a light and sound signal, but also a signifier, a word. In the second part of the experiment, they "serve" the animal only the word, which is enough for saliva and its gastric juices to flow.

* * *

Can we, finally, reduce the gap between Freud's formula, that of the cannibalistic devouring of the father, and that of eating the Book? Some remarks and the little apologue that follow attempt to achieve this.

The canonical books of the monotheistic religions, those that occupy the place of the Book—the Old Testament and the Talmud for the Jews, the Gospels for the Christians, the Koran for the Muslims—have at least one point in common: the historic condition of their re-

Chapter 6

daction. Each of these master works retraces an experience of conversion, that is to say, of subjective mutation, the total overhaul of a world view. Curiously, the transcription of this has never taken place *in statu nascendi*, at the moment in which the experience is occurring, but rather once it ends, by its last actors. It is their *testament*.

Thus the last Talmudic masters, Ravina and Rab Achi, write the Talmud when the Jewish dispersion, though not completely carried out, has entered the realm of fact. Similarly, the Evangelists report the saga of Christ only *a posteriori*. The Sanhedrin establishes the Biblical canon when the institutions of the former Hebrew state reach their end. Further examples may be adduced. The most luminous is no doubt that of Moses entrusting his book to the Elders shortly before his end.

The effect of "putting into a book" a teaching at the moment in which its historical hour is being eclipsed, is in its death-throes, results in the conserving, suspending of this discourse in an extra-temporal existence, in a nearly *hypnotic* fixity, a waking dream. The book thus structures the group within which it is born, gives it its bond, and ensures its perpetuation.

For the remote descendent of this book a second reality exists. It may at times look unreal and yet it is as real as things that happened yesterday: the silhouette of Isaac always stands out in the dusk moving ahead of the caravan that brings the betrothed from Mesopotamia who "will console" him "for his mother." There is Jacob watering the flocks of the young Rachel, the fire-storm on Sinai, the solitary ascent of Mount Nebo, David and his harp, Isaiah's imprecations; all pass as though I today, amid suburban traffic jams or waiting at an airport, and were the direct witnesses of those majestic scenes, strange mirages that nothing dispels, the solid core of my memory and of my phantasm.

Is this, then, the meta-real phenomenon the poet Edgar Allan Poe intuited in his tale "The Facts in the Case of M. Valdemar"?[112]

In this 'extraordinary story,' the hero, at the moment of passing away, has himself hypnotized, and dies in that state. The hypnosis keeps the body from decomposing, while the dead man retains the

---

[112] Edgar Allan Poe, *Collected Works of Edgar Allan Poe, vol. III*, (Cambridge: Harvard University Press, 1978).

faculty of speech and testifies to his terrible experience. Ultimately he will plead for the hypnosis to end, whereupon his cadaver liquefies into an abominable state of rot.

The Book gives reality to Poe's metaphor. It keeps alive, despite its being a thing of the past, the word of the founding masters of its respective group. Eating it takes us back to that atrocious cannibalistic feast that Freud imagined in his totemic meal.

* * *

Thus, literally, the Book appears as the necessary specter that haunts men. Around it we could spin a new conception of History, of which it would be, the true hidden mover, no less than the class struggle, Cleopatra's nose, or technical progress. Let's settle for a few remarks that will provisionally finish off our weaving.

The history of men actually seems to us to be sewn by the thread of the Book, by its ferret-like circulation in the social fabric, by the parsing of human space into the rival groups it creates.

At the very interior of the cultural spaces determined and structured by these books, indefinite struggles to the death occur, struggles not of pure prestige but for control of the Book, to possess its repository and gain control over its circulation, and—in the game of games— to impose a certain official reading. In a word, the Book presents itself as the true scepter of power.

Doesn't contesting established power often revert to translating differently the canonical Scriptures, altering the perspective on them in a reworking so profound that the language itself may be modified? I can cite, as an exemplary illustration, Luther's great adventure as the true inventor of modern German.

This aspiration to control the Book is clearly an aspiration to tyranny, to hold in one's hands the networks passed down from authority and have at one's mercy the metabolism of the *jouissance* of the flock to whom one appoints oneself as guide, now out of harm's way, spared any further ordeal.

Ezekiel's luminous lesson stands at the opposite pole. He who eats the Book, by an individual and inalienable possession, eludes this economy of tyranny. The Book *is his*, directly, with no intercessor or guide. It becomes hard bone, where sometimes the teeth of the great mouth get broken and always meet with resistance. The prophet is op-

Chapter 6

posed to the tyrant in this relation to this swallowed Book, while the latter has it guarded, put on the index, hidden in some strong-room where no one can get to it.

An essential organ of power—at any rate of a power careful to perpetuate itself, and not some limited exercise of pure violence—this property of the Book keeps to its role in the mechanism of transmission.

Among the great tasks that an institution, a power, must resolve, the most important is that of its transmission, of the perpetuation of its structure.[113] Out of this routinely come thorny issues of inheritance, the source of violent conflicts, caused by the fierce coveting of the Book.

The great institutions that Freud took as models, the Church and the army, present this exemplary character of having nearly perfectly mastered this delicate operation. Such is not the case with the institutions of psychoanalysis themselves.

---

[113] The underlying question here is obviously that of filiation.

PART THREE

THE BOOK AND THE CLINIC

CHAPTER 1

BEYOND A CLINIC OF ORALITY

Psychoanalysis, first and foremost a praxis, demands that all speculation within its domain be gauged against the real of its clinic. Does this permit a finer grasp, an elucidation of phenomena that have remained obscure? A test against which we must henceforth measure ourselves, by exhibiting its true dimension, even if it was never absent from previous developments.

Clinical material would clearly not be lacking, considering the fundamental place that the oral drive occupies in all psychopathological structures.

Certainly we think first, and legitimately so, of those in which the oral drive comes to the fore: alcoholism and anorexia, for instance.

But beyond that, if it is true, as we say after Freud, that man founds and assimilates the symbolic through his orality, then our path must soon cross the issue of troubles with language acquisition.

Dyslexia, a child's inability to learn to read, or to do so only after a thousand difficulties, and a veritable plague in contemporary education, is of special interest to us.

The psychoanalyst encounters dyslexia either in direct observation of the child, or in the anamnesis, during treatment of an adult. In a paradox familiar to the clinician, this second path proves more informative than direct observation.

This isolated trouble in the subject's entry into the symbolic becomes the essential element in psychosis. We shall see what an unexpected reinforcement to our construction even a cursory look at schizophrenia gives us.

My thesis, moreover, as a complementary illumination of various psychopathological questions, allows me to glimpse how a certain ailment can be transformed into another.

The practitioner no doubt is scarcely surprised to see, for example, anorexia episodically become bulimia—Maimonides would already have located these two troubles on the same *mida*, the same "straight line" of pathology. It is more novel to posit an adult ethylism and a childhood dyslexia as proceeding from the same cause.

Other questions arise for us. Foremost is the question of a *psychological theory of medication*. All doctors know that beyond its pharmaceutical effect, one often observes that a pill or potion frequently creates paradoxical, at times disproportionate effects. The question culminates in the *placebo* effect: perceived cures observed daily from medically inactive products. The results obtained by homeopathic therapeutics might well be explained in this way.

This strange effect gains in scope with the psychosomatic ailments which, quite unlike troubles referred to as functional, present confirmed somatic injuries.

It is easy to verify; the terrain to survey here is immense. Unable to establish a detailed summary, I'll insist instead on certain points that by now seem connected:

—Schizophrenia as an extreme, 'outer-limit' trouble in the individual's relation to the symbolic.
—Dyslexia, inversely, as a first, limited manifestation of this trouble.
—Alcoholism as a privileged question, the one that undoubtedly provides the best materials for our study.
—The neuroses, the territory par excellence of psychoanalysis.
—Some general remarks about a psychological theory of medication.

I have preferred to use published documents, which anyone can verify.

In my view this group forms a first clinical stratum upon which my construction may be established.

CHAPTER 2

PROOF FROM THE SCHIZO

It is commonly said that psychotics—madmen—lay bare their unconscious. It's an erroneous statement, yet one that's stuck in people's minds because it accounts for immediate, and poorly interpreted, data of observation.

In psychosis, the psychic manifestations, the formations of the unconscious take on a rigid, quasi-petrified, non-dialectic character. The comparison often used is that of a film that's suddenly frozen on one image, turned into a still photo—which, however, makes the observation and study of this formation less complicated.

In every subject a sort of basic translation has been carried out, a *metaphor*, that is, the substitution of one term for another, the second one veiling the first: the desire *of* the mother and *for* the mother is transmuted by the function of the father that has now become the keystone of psychic reality. With the psychotic, this principle translation has not been made.

Such, quite briefly, is the currently prevalent psychoanalytic conception worked out by Lacan from the theories that Freud established in his famous commentary on the memoirs of the psychotic Schreber.

In the flood of analytic literature devoted to Schreber's work —and Freud's commentary—one detail has never been underlined to the extent it warrants. It now takes on a singular importance: namely, that Schreber *writes a book*, whereupon his troubles grow calm enough for the medical authorities to accept his release from the asylum. A manifestation, in an extreme case, of the therapeutic character—hesitant and incomplete, to be sure—of book writing.

A psychotic is a person for whom the paternal function is like a hole, without signification in the unconscious. To the question, "What is a father?" comes no answer but delirium.

Chapter 2

We have patiently established the equivalence, Talmudically inspired and by now fundamental:

book = child

For certain subjects, to write a book offsets the gap that punctures the symbolic network. The book becomes an imperfect, frail "stopgap measure" to be renewed, but which plugs up the psychic infirmity that comes from a deficiency in the paternal function.

This outlet of writing a book—and not just any little book but one that aims to be a definitive work like the one Schreber thought he was creating, the book of books, approaching the status of *the* Book—turns out to be extremely frequent on examination; it turns up whenever a subject falters before his task as a man, a father *confronted with the ascendency of feminine desire.*

The pathological figures vary; among them, the eminent one is the alcoholic. In its multiple forms, the question remains one of psychosis.[114]

A text less well-known than Schreber's, *le Schizo et les langues*[115] (*The Schizo and Languages*) by Louis Wolfson, broadly confirms these propositions. Few documents so well illustrate the relation between psychosis and language structure.

Louis Wolfson, author and main hero of his book, presents himself as a schizophrenic who has undergone numerous psychiatric hospitalizations. His whole life revolves around this work (written directly in French with some remarkable oddities of style). The end of the book attests to a certain improvement in his illness.

Thus, once again, an individual subject to the most severe psychic disorders finds in writing a book—which, in the author's ambition, aims at nothing less than reforming language in its writing and its grammar, making it therefore a sort of canonical book—release from the distress that came of the absence of this elementary translation a father performs. All of Wolfson's activity consists precisely in a frantic effort at translation.

---

[114] Lacan presented a convergent argument in relation to Joyce and his oeuvre, a prosthesis to psychosis, without however making recourse to the category of the Book.

[115] Louis Wolfson, *le Schizo et les langues*, (Paris: Gallimard, 1970).

Louis Wolfson is an American Jew, though for his family that reference has lost all importance. The commentaries that the book has elicited barely lay emphasis on this fact that seems essential, the very site of the foreclosure of the Name-of-the-Father. The hero's incredible activity, devoted especially to the study of Hebrew, will shed a pale light on this primordial signifier.

His particularly meager biography is quickly summed up in the first pages of the book. The child of a couple very soon divorced, with a sad, wretched history: an especially colorless father who could fairly be said not to exist, an illustration of what the Lacanian term of foreclosure can cover when so embodied. His relation to his son is summed up in visits to the psychiatric hospital that end with the gift of a coin.

Still, one incident in his childhood gives us pause: the first trouble that the child L.W. manifested turned out to be a serious case of dyslexia. "To be able to read this language to an acceptable degree," he writes, referring to himself in the third person, "that, had been a true struggle for him."[116]

The "schizo"—another name he gives himself—thus verifies the *law of transformation between pathological disturbances*, here, between aberrant eating habits, dyslexia, and psychosis.

Wolfson's book, contrary to other texts in this genre, is not the transcription of some great delirium, of hallucinatory interpretations, but rather the minute description of the activities of this person, activities that come under two headings.

First is the linguistic heading. The main trouble for Wolfson, who lives in New York, is that he can't bear to hear even a single word of English, especially when spoken by his mother. Thus he lives with his fingers stuck in his ears or wears headphones that connect him to foreign broadcasts. Yet this stringent barrier isn't entirely soundproof; sometimes an English word crosses it, causing intense pain. To clear his consciousness of the intruding signifier, Wolfson has come up with a curious linguistic process, consisting of translating it into several foreign languages, each translation having to contain certain consonants of the English word, to offer him a vague homophony. For him, only the consonants matter, a vague echo of his Hebraic ties.

---

[116] L. Wolfson, *op. cit.*, 24.

Chapter 2

The book is almost entirely devoted to these draining and seemingly ridiculous linguistic activities. The author expends formidable energy on them, while at the same time, and not without results—as his book written directly in French attests—he studies languages as hard as Russian, French, Hebrew, and several others. To sample the style of these exercises, a reading of several pages of the book is indispensable.

These strange translations began after an intervention of his father's, mendacious yet the only one no doubt made in the spirit of his son, declaring that the English word "tree" was the same in Russian. Wolfson will cling to this grotesque remark, this word from his father, as though to a life buoy.

The second category of Wolfson's pathological activity is his eating habits. Abetted by mother, the "schizo" periodically indulges in crazy compulsive bulimias, carried out with an extreme excitement, binges that leave him with a great, guilty despondency.

The precise description of the onset of these attacks is a unique document of exceptional clinical interest to us. First there's a preliminary phase, an anxious expectation, from which Wolfson attempts to protect himself with a shield familiar to us by now: books.

"The emotional need to take one or even several books with him when going to eat (as well as when just going anywhere)."[117]

A testimony that confirms those provided by analytic treatment or mere observation: the book calms anxiety, not only by being read but also by its sheer presence.

Thus, a patient of mine was in the habit, after certain sessions, of going into a bookshop and buying a book, or into a pastry shop, with a preference for *millefeuilles* (literally: a thousand leaves). In my native country (Tunisia), among devout families, children suffering from night fears were advised to put one or more books of the Torah under their pillow. No anxiety of my childhood ever held up to this treatment, which Wolfson was thus familiar with, and yet proves to be an inadequate screen for him.

The second characteristic of Wolfson's food orgies is just as important. It isn't a matter of those eating excesses but, literally, of filling

---

[117] L. Wolfson, op. cit. p. 49.

the buccal cavity to the gullet, such that *the least interstice*—the spaces between the lips, cheeks and teeth—is eliminated.

"Stuffing one's mouth with big pieces of food," he writes, "up to the neglected spaces between his teeth and not to be able any more to close that organ," up to the point that saliva can no longer flow freely in that volume in which every interval has been filled.

Aren't we confronted here with the opposite, the negation of the protocol of every rite and dietary myth the *kashrut* teaches? In opposition to the meticulous care every culture takes to transform the continuum of the alimentary bolus into a discontinuous order in which the intervals between elements are as broad as possible, the psychotic, being out-of-discourse, aims to reestablish the continuum and erase the symbolic.

That the mechanism of these aberrations should be the rejection of eating-the-Book and of its surrogate reading is proved by Wolfson's remarkable description. His bulimic crises are in fact accompanied by an apparently unrelated phenomenon: avoiding at all cost reading the labels glued on the cans and boxes of foods!

No doubt it is this rejection of writing that Wolfson displaces into a hallucinatory phobia, that of tiny worms and the eggs of parasites—lines [*traits*] and punctuation marks—that might pollute the food he eats.

As Gilles Deleuze notes in his penetrating preface to the book, Wolfson's psychic reality rests on the equation:

$$words = food$$

The psychotic openly reveals an operation the rest of us carry out unconsciously.

Yet no human being, not even a totally mad one, could manage long to survive a complete collapse of the symbolic. *Le Schizo et les langues* is the tale of heroic and laughable efforts to set up poor props against this collapse, and raise them once again when they have been swept away; to reestablish, in a word, the abolished structure.

The first of these displays is a mental compulsion to analyze chemically everything he eats. The study of *kashrut*—that, once again!—already revealed the existence and importance of this phenomenon that creates or reinforces the separations, the discontinuous.

Chapter 2

The same wish to reestablish a discrete order is evident in Wolfson's dietary choices beyond his bulimic crises, choices that underscore how narrow the link is between cuisine and the symbolic. We read:

> The psychotic assumed that eating bread, cakes, fried shrimp and other dishes to which one would add vegetable oil, *truly unsaturated*, for cooking or frying, was healthy for him or at least did not harm him as much as if animal fat (this being *saturated*) were to be used in cooking.[118]

The medical reasons Wolfson adduces to justify this search for the unsaturated, however true they may be, seem in this context secondary rationalizations. The incredible lengths he goes to, hacking at letters and signifiers, tend precisely to develop this unsaturation. The privileged tool of this operation, the book, naturally meets up with its privileged form, ersatz of the Bible, the *dictionary*. Wolfson uses a host of them, they surround him, protect him.

Explicitly stating the equivalence, so painfully established, between reading and eating, he writes, "And just as it was often difficult for the sick young man to stop eating once he had begun, so it was equally hard to stop consulting his dictionaries in foreign languages once he had begun with them."[119]

His effort is not in vain. Little by little, Wolfson loosens the grip that is killing him, and the end of his book shows that his relation to his family, to the world, to the English language becomes bearable.

Indisputably, Wolfson's merit is great in contributing this rough, irrefutable testimony to the strange relations that man maintains with language and the alimentary sphere. Eating one, he swallows the other.

---

[118] L. Wolfson, *op. cit.*, 52-53.
[119] *Ibid.*, 212.

CHAPTER 3

THE DYSLEXIC AND HIS FATHER

If we assert the existence of a profound relation of the father to the Book, this is not to say that the nature of that relation strikes us as any less profoundly enigmatic. The Scriptures that declare the eternal coexistence of God and the Torah take us back to this enigma, to the difficulty, for example, of setting up a hierarchy between these terms. A possible substitution of the one for the other, thus a similarity of consistency, is a directly perceptible first manifestation—let us recall the feeling of security that both provide.

The importance of the real father in carrying out the Book's incorporation, which results in mastery of written language, is a second manifestation.

The study of failures, if not of impossibilities of the acquisition, dyslexia itself finds its natural place here. No doubt the materials with which we will deal don't have the desirable breadth, and these several pages form merely an introduction to this important question.

Let us recall that two paths are open to investigation: the direct one, the child, that is, and the indirect one: the "subproduct" of an adult analysis, which reestablishes a link with the preferences of Freud himself. This second path is indisputably richer, allowing us to better perceive the connections and transformations of this disturbance into another. Yet the practitioner, beholden to the framework of treatment, cannot conduct and intensify his investigation as he might like.

Direct examination of the dyslexic child is ostensibly more promising. A consultation in a children's health center is enough for encountering a high number of cases, since dyslexia constitutes one of the main symptoms encountered today in child psychiatry and of the most common motives for consultation.

Yet the reasons opposing a true psychoanalytic investigation are also very numerous. The request for a consultation comes more or

Chapter 3

less invariably from the school. The teachers, faced with this difficulty, more and more commonly feel an anxiety-provoking impotence. The age of the children is a second obstacle. Between seven and ten years, in what is called the latency period, the moment does not seem propitious or productive for undertaking a psychotherapy which, most often, the children themselves don't want. They no longer have the facility of the very small child to enter into the play of children's cures and haven't yet formulated the desire an adult, or even certain adolescents, can convey.

Added to these unfavorable conditions are, certainly, internal reasons that have to do with the trouble itself, and with the family structure of which it is an effect, and which function as a veto to analysis.

Also, the interlocutor assumed to be "natural" for the dyslexic is not the analyst—"What good will that do?" the child often echoes his family in asking—but rather the speech therapist.

These pessimistic considerations must be carefully balanced against the personality and the know-how the therapist possesses with respect to children. They will not prevent me, however, from venturing to make the following observation.

The analysts who deal with dyslexia have often placed children's mistakes in reading or writing in the category of the Freudian lapsus or "failed" act (*acte manqué*), in the sense that it successfully manifests a repressed desire. This path proves sterile.

The dyslexic mistake *falls shy* of being the lapsus that, in order to occur, implies a psychic inscription of the signifying battery of language. Only then can one term replace another. In the case of this child, the very position of the symbolic is in question. Whence the difficulty for the analyst of grasping the symptom.

At least the present elaboration better enables identifying its nature. What it involves is a failing, serious at times, in "apprenticeship," the acquisition of the symbolic in its materiality, that of the letter and of writing. The mechanisms described earlier, those by which the discontinuous emerges from the continuous, have functioned poorly, and areas of continuousness exist where an interval should have been formed. Consequently, the pure difference between two letters in some close written form isn't perceived. The context of signification may compensate for this failing, which permits a "global approach." Yet isolated, the letter, as a pure symbol with no signified, becomes barely decipherable. The dyslexic has not entirely—or, in extreme cases, has not at all—eaten the Book.

This structural conception, briefly presented in the hope that practitioners confronted with such tasks will come up with something more advanced and more probing, is complemented by a second, more concrete one: the failure to acquire the letter has to do with the dyslexic's particular relation to the father.

Before defining it, and to avoid misunderstandings, we must recall that the position of the father is always untenable. Freud never ceased hammering this home—he for whom the ideal father was the dead father. It has become extremely difficult to occupy this place in our world destructured by a science that smashes to bits the prostheses of millennia. The dyslexic's father is at best a rough sketch, or, in the case of Wolfson, where dyslexia is the harbinger of a psychosis, he simply absconds.

Theories have flourished over the last years, placing the pathogenesis on the side of mothers. How many studies and speculations about the mother of schizophrenics, anorexics, etc.! However interesting they might be, they miss the essential element of Freudian and Lacanian thought: the pathogeny is always, in the final analysis, on the side of the father, who has shirked his task. The mothers do what they can and undoubtedly sometimes complicate or create obstacles for the action of the father, yet the latter's responsibility remains entire. The mother's pathogeny, often incriminated, on close inspection, proves to be induced, secondary to a dizzying inadequacy of the father. The typology of mother following a nosographic framework ought to be replaced by—if only this sort of exercise had any value at all!—a paternal typology. The personality of the dyslexic's father would be easy to identify.

At issue here is the absent father, a *materialized* absence. This is the opposite of the neurotic's father, characterized as deficient, whose disordered efforts, and occasional authoritarianism, poorly mask a frequent inconsistency and incoherence of principles, exhausting him at a task he carries out badly, but which he does carry out. He differs, too, from the father of the psychotic, often present if not omnipresent, but with a dizzying symbolic inefficacy. The dyslexic's father simply isn't there.

When I was starting out in this profession, whenever a dyslexic child accompanied by his mother would arrive for a consultation, I would systematically ask to meet the father. In several dozens of cases, there came *only* polite refusals: "he" was very tired at night after coming home from work; "he" didn't have the time and, if the invitation turned into an imperative, preferred that his offspring stop treatment. In short, "he" didn't get involved.

The explanations of the mothers, very much alike despite the variety of the cases, always formed the same profile and same scenario: the father, when he came home evenings, would want to look in on his children when they were already asleep. One woman summed up the question like this: "You know, my husband's one of those dads who've given up."

Thus the necessary encounter between father and child could not *materially* occur. To hell with subtle neurotic misconceptions and misunderstandings! At the extreme, when the father comes home the kids are sleeping and tomorrow, when they're going off to school, they'll have to make sure not to wake up their progenitor exhausted from an effort that in fact has never begun.

The treatment of a young woman, A., revealed and identical set of conditions. She was five years old when her father disappeared one day. Was it really necessary, furthermore, for this father of four children, neither to leave nor to send a farewell or explanatory letter, and never at any point give a clue to where on this planet he might be? Fifteen years later our patient, with the same desperation, was still unsure whether her father was dead or alive and where he had lived. Quite soon after he took off, she had suffered from a severe case of dyslexia treated by a long speech-therapy retraining.

This dyslexia would later give way to anxiety-inducing fits of bulimia that, without reaching Wolfsonian extremes, upset her greatly. The whole family history strangely bears this orality as a stigma, at times psychosomatic: A.'s missing father and her brother are severely diabetic.

A. interrupted her analysis after a few months, unable, she said, to tolerate the fits of despair into which each session would plunge her.

It seems risky to deduce from these fragmentary remarks a therapeutic conduct for the scholastic plague that dyslexia is today. Yet it also seems advantageous to elucidate its true dimension, linked to modern family structure, where the weakening of the father's authority and prestige is of a piece with that of the Book, benefiting only the hypertrophy of the imaginary the audio-visual media have brought on.

CHAPTER 4

MEDICATION AND PSYCHOSOMATICS

Surely one of the unexpected perspectives that our thesis opens up is to be found here. If man eats writing and persists in this act it is surely because he derives some benefit from it, especially for his health. Thus in one stroke we touch on the theory —virtually nonexistent— of a psychology of medications and of psychosomatics.

The principle behind the psychology of medication is easy to state: the name of the medication plays a role, and perhaps a decisive one, in a given medication's therapeutic success. In the act of swallowing some pill with a name, the sick person swallows the writing of that name, much like the Jew at the *seder* of Rosh Hashanah.

Let us add that the Chinese have known this for ages, since the ideogram *yào*, which denotes medication, breaks down into these sub-characters: eat – paper – language.

The importance of the name of the medication as such escapes the attention of no physician and enters day-to-day experience, in general medicine as well as, with particular clarity, in psychiatry. I can cite the case of a psychotic vehemently refusing his Danetol tablets, "because they were doing him harm," while accepting every other medication of the same family. In conversation he ended up confiding, "I feel damned [*damné*] enough without swallowing that damn thing, too [*danéchose*]."

A woman patient had a penchant for *Marinoctyl*;[120] reading it as *nuit de noces*, "marriage night," she thought it could only favor her marrying. Many more such examples could be given.

---

[120] I have altered the names of these well-known medications.

Chapter 4

Once again, what the psychotic crudely formulates hovers in the background, unconsciously, in every relation of a subject to medications that for ages have been taken only orally.

The preceding examples have a deliberately generalizing character. The link with the name of the medication, its power of suggestion, is usually much more subtle and personalized, tied to a group of letters, a cipher, or number, perhaps in the way that Wolfson carried out his translations.

Drug marketing experts have understood the phenomenon for a long time. Companies no longer issue a new medication, unless it's some truly effective, new molecule, without lavishing great attention on the product's name.

Beyond the pharmacopeia, many food products, especially candies, use the same ploys.

Jean Guir thinks that psychosomatic illnesses might be triggered by the absorption of a signifier linked to the traumatic events of the subject's family history. Conversely, in prescribing placebos that have names specifically composed according to this history, he might have prompted the disappearance of certain skin conditions.[121] Here we touch, very cautiously, on a "real" that the marabouts of Senegal and traditional medicines have manipulated for ages and ages.

For centuries, medicine has perhaps done nothing other than administrate some signifier to swallow, one which it took care to formulate in Latin, thus shrouding it in mystery and religion.

Scientific medicine believes it can reduce the reliance on the power of suggestion. Paradoxically, it has exacerbated the demand in this direction under the heading of "soft" medicines: herbalism (phytotherapy), homeopathy, etc.

At the risk of stirring up a controversy, I attribute the effects of this latter to the considerable wealth of signifiers—with Latin and with Kabbalistic ciphers, at that—that homeopathy manipulates.

These half-magical, half-amusing phenomena in any case illustrate—albeit partially—the place that the Book occupies in the psychosomatic illnesses, real, often serious illnesses, in which psychic factors, for instance the loss of a loved one, contribute to their overdetermined onset.

---

[121] Jean Guir, *Psychosomatique et Cancer*, (Paris: Point Hors Ligne, 1983).

CHAPTER 5

THE ALCOHOLIC

Alcoholism appears to be the richest and most propitious clinical structure for exploring the relation of the human being to writing. We know the eminent place alcoholics occupy in literature, and some of the best literature at that, the kind that warrants the same capital letter as in Book.

The preceding theoretical elaborations owe a lot to the examination of this question, and we must briefly resituate them.

A preliminary word about methodology. The following study rests exclusively on two great literary oeuvres.

Another, more habitual way might have been tried, the psycho-biographical, at times improperly called psychoanalytic, searching through the events of a life for the determinants of an oeuvre. It's a method that occasionally yields something not without interest: we learn, say, that Fitzgerald would not drink when he was at work on one of his great novels.

Yet we must refuse the temptations inherent in this procedure. It hasn't the fecundity it would appear to have and the arguments it adduces remain debatable.

There's another harder but more promising approach: the intrinsic analysis of the written work itself. It is to the work itself that a genuine writer entrusts his unsolvable questions, his holes in the real, his truth—stamped, to be sure, with several different seals. Yet these can only hone the ingenuity of the decipherer.

So, confronted with an oeuvre, the decipherer has the chance to construct another work of some value, instead of a vague, at times unwholesome, line of inquiry.

The hypothesis of our labor here is the following: the suffering that leads a subject to alcohol derives from his relation to the feminine

Chapter 5

sex, from the insurmountable questions that this relation poses for him, primarily that of being a father.

Let's spell out at last what we are to understand by this paternal function discovered by Freud. The triad Lacan introduced under the categories of the Real, the Symbolic, and the Imaginary allows a better grasp of these articulations.

A father's function is in effect triple. From its very outset, psychoanalysis laid stress on the great novelty, the barrier to incestuous desire that he sets up. This disjunction of the mother and her progeny founds the symbolic order, the regulator of alliances.[122]

Later Freud discovered a second level, not without connections with the first, yet nevertheless isolable. That of narcissism and its consequences: the deathly rivalry with the brother, or rather the Lacanian dimension of the Imaginary. The word of the father here must still echo the formidable commandment issued at Sinai: *Thou shalt not kill!*

To these two registers, so familiar today, is added a third, perhaps more essential. That of the Real, defined as the impossible, and first of all as impossible to utter. The scriptural trace of it is preserved in Moses' famous dialogue with the Burning Bush. To the question of His Name, God answers: "I am That I am," thus signifying that there is something of the unspeakable, the impossible, whose function it ensures.

A father's deficiency necessarily affects these three planes, as everything in the clinic attests to, although only one aspect or another may predominate. The trilogy of psychoses—paranoia, schizophrenia, mania—is surely tied up to this fact.

To all problematics of the All, to oceanic feelings as well as cosmic aspirations, to all the fun-house halls of mirrors our age seems to have taken such a fancy to, the father is he who says no. How might a subject who has become Father utter this word except as a swindler, a con man, if he himself can't make the renunciations it implies?

To procreate, it has been said, is to accept one's death, the transitory character of existence. Yet it is also to accept the interval, short

---

[122] C. Lévi-Strauss, *Structures élémentaires de la parenté, The Elementary Structures of Kinship*, trans. James Harle Bell, (London: Eyre & Spottiswoode, 1969), *op. cit.*

as it may be, of one's own life. To make a pact with life and accept one's death has, despite appearances, nothing contradictory about it.

The alcoholic accepts neither the one nor the other, nor, consequently, their disjunction. In fact, he hurtles into this death that terrifies him beyond reason.

The desire of the Other, of the woman, to which he must respond by mediating it, is a dizzying abyss for him. Is this as it is for the psychotic? No, not quite the same way.

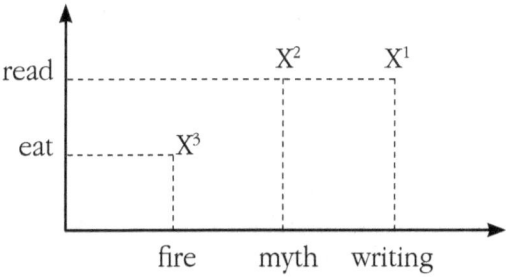

Figure no. 12

In the clinical space defined at the end of the second part of this book, the position X^1 (*book x writing*) represents the ideal point that surely no one ever reaches except asymptotically, that of the desiring subject.

In not getting there, the alcoholic "turns back," like a routed army, to positions easier to hold. Toward point X^2, where the neurotic cozily settles into his individual myth? Yes, he does strive there for a time, even spinning out yarns and myths. Yet his balancing point is at X^3 (*eating x fire*). Instead of eating or reading the Book, an access to paternity, he can incorporate only its primitive form, fire, this burning fire that alcohol brings him.[123]

Someone may try to dislodge the alcoholic from this place. A woman, for instance. He then expresses the wish, ever so faint, to

---

[123] I should also mention addiction to smoking, so often associated. This analysis converges, with that of Midrash, on the couple: man + woman (*Ich* + *Icha*). If we remove from these names the letters of the divine name (the Father), there remains only *Ech:* "fire."

Chapter 5

break out of his intoxication and to enter into paternity in his relationship with his woman. Yet what chance path allows access to a position untenable for him? Precisely our "repair patch," the Book.

If *child* has an equivalent in the signifier *book*, then writing, making a book, becomes an acclimatization, a foundation course for paternity, a special form of couvade. A compelling desire to write—*pruritus calami*, as the phrase goes—is triggered in certain subjects at the approach of that crucial moment, especially as adolescence turns into adulthood.

The alcoholic, whether real or still only potential, is thus particularly marked out for writing, interposing his creations in the slender space that keeps him from the abyss.

This analysis rests on the reading of a great novel, *Under the Volcano*, by Malcolm Lowry.[124]

Lowry was an alcoholic, as he himself admitted, and his great work traces the drama of an alcoholic, the Consul. Thus, confronted with his own words, we have the choice between psychobiography and the study of his book, or a mix of the two. The advantage of just examining texts seems evident, so greatly does their richness outweigh that of the biographical elements one can glean from them.

Under the Volcano, like a classical drama, recounts *one* day in the life of one character, the Consul, who is reaching the farthest limits of ethylism: indeed, the one day is his last day. In this brief interval of time, the elements of his existence take their definitive place.

Every true destiny is carried out in the encounter with a woman, and the consul does not lack his own. It falls to this partner to reveal the crux of the drama.

The Consul passionately loves his wife, Yvonne; yet he can neither recognize her as such, nor give her the child she desires, nor, conversely, separate from her. Everything seems wedged into this interstice. The wife thinks she'll be able to break this in-between state by a lapse into adultery.

There is no such thing as sexual relation, as Lacan would hammer home, meaning that there is no conjunction, no sort of least common denominator existing between the two sexes. Coitus, in its very *jouissance*, is merely a lure that masks this radical and tragic disjunc-

---

[124] Reading this book, for those who haven't done so, is essential.

The Alcoholic

tion. The couple of the Consul and Yvonne verifies this impossibility. A pathological couple? Absolutely, yet their pathology has to do not with the impossibility of their relation but rather their inability to bear this universal.

Lowry illustrates the crucial issues of his book by intensifying them with references to the mineral world. Since the tale unfolds in Mexico, the silhouettes of the two majestic volcanoes loom over the landscape: Popocatepetl and Ixtaccihuatl, volcanoes that, in Aztec mythology, form a pair of spouses irreparably separated by a fault yet infinitely close. Each aspires to, and weeps for not being able to, conjoin with the other.

As it happens, Lowry draws this symbol from a source that, by his own claim, sustains his entire literary construction: the Kabbalah. Didn't Lacan himself say that it was necessary to read the Kabbalah to understand this law of the absence of a sexual relation? The primary theme of the esoteric Jewish texts is in fact this problem of human sexuality, marked as it is by a structural flaw.

Why can't the Consul bear this common fate? In a brief passage, Lowry depicts the hero's childhood—childhood, that always exemplary moment, less for its determinism in pathology than for the way it so clearly manifests the relations of a subject to his structure and to his progenitors. The relation of the Consul to his father was altogether inconsistent. Despite the ellipses of the text, we can sense the "weight" of this inconsistency, different from the deficiency of the neurotic's father, but close, rather, to the absence noted among dyslexics, a structure akin to the alcoholic's.

This paternal inconsistency wreaks its havoc not only on the plane of sexual interrelations, but also on the two others described earlier.

If the father's inconsistency exacerbates the question of incest, paralyzing the hero in his love, it also unleashes a deadly fraternal rivalry.

It is said of the Consul, a former naval officer, that in his youth, during the First World War, he killed a group of German prisoners and threw them into his ship's boiler.

Yvonne will tie together the two planes of relation to the woman and to the brother. The Consul in fact has a brother, who grows smitten with his sister-in-law. Lowry will avoid making him her lover, a role he reserves for a character erased from the novel, Laruelle. None-

Chapter 5

theless, Hugh potentially occupies that place, the author having doubled up one role—a fundamental mechanism in the imaginary register.

Yvonne's fall takes on an exceptional gravity, for it plunges the Consul into alcoholism, into that oral regression in which the mouth of the subject, in a bottomless hunger-thirst, becomes the image in the mirror of the angst-provoking Other ready to swallow him up.

To this Other, the place of the Symbolic where, for the Consul, the father did not come to mark his limit, Lowry has given a body, that of nature. Just as the figure of the two volcanoes represents the archetype of the couple, the mouth of the Other is materialized by the constant presence of a dizzying ravine, a sewer, the *barranca*, which, at the end of the story will swallow up the Consul's body before he is quite dead, as it simultaneously swallows up a dead dog, and as it seems ready to swallow up everything. The Consul can endure this anxiety-provoking unleashing of the Imaginary only through alcohol.

There remains the plane of the Real, that of the impossibility of utterance, the failure of which produces the ethylic delirium, the mad discourse that will entail the death of the Consul, arrested as a spy by a group of soldiers and finished off in the *barranca* where the knot of destiny is fastened once and for all.

Yet before this ignoble end, the hero has struggled, has searched for a way out— once more, the way of the Book.

In the long explanatory letter to his publisher that serves as a preface to the novel, Lowry says that his text sinks its deep roots into the Jewish Kabbalah which "represents man's spiritual aspiration," and that its plan is inspired by the Zohar, a fact even a well-informed and careful reader might scarcely perceive without this avowal.

This subtle reference underscores the slender hope that riddles the book at one point: if only the Consul could write a book! Not just any book, but an absolute book, the Book, which would be the quintessence of the Kabbalah.

Indisputably, the hero is aware of the place of his deficiency and wants, like Joyce, to overcome it by himself producing the missing piece. Oddly enough, Yvonne, the wife, a woman so practical, seemingly so ill-equipped for esoteric speculation, supports this idea, perceiving the truth of it with her woman's intuition.

Yet the attempt fails, indeed doesn't even begin, as though gripped by an absolute inhibition. The hero presents a sort of hemorrhaging hole too wide to be stitched back up and therefore avert tragedy.

The Alcoholic

* * *

This analysis of *Under the Volcano*, if only for its rapidity, raises a number of objections. The novel, it can be said, contains few indices of the link between alcohol and the Book, even if the function and hope that the project of writing represents for the hero are real.

The link with alcohol is obviously my interpretation, and legitimate, only— if provided with some shred of proof.

To provide such proof "before the fact," the failure to ingest the Book is nearly impossible. Yet wouldn't an attempt to adduce such proof "after the fact,"—that is, to show that the Consul would have been able to recover if he had in fact written his book of books—be just as desperate?

It would be, if another great poet, in one of his best plays, hadn't provided us with this proof at the same time as the counter-proof: Ibsen, who in his drama *Hedda Gabler*, expands upon the question *Under the Volcano* raises.

Ibsen should certainly occupy a privileged place in the readings of every analyst. Freud, his contemporary, certainly thought so, placing him almost on the same level as Sophocles and Shakespeare. He himself wrote penetrating commentaries on *The Wild Duck* and *Rosmersholm*, emphasizing the poet's extreme psychological rigor and finesse.

Too often people wrongly view Ibsen simply as a critic of the social mores and the prudery of his time. His real importance has to do with the acuity of his insight into the unconscious.

Hedda Gabler calls into play virtually all the nodal points that concern us: alcohol, childbirth, the book. Its structure is relatively simple, that of a quadrille of two men and two women, always in mirror-reflection.

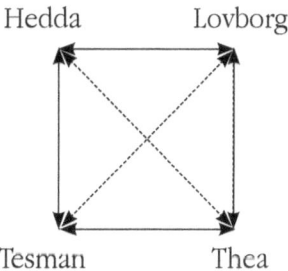

Figure no. 13

Chapter 5

To these four characters are added a few others, secondary in terms of their presence on the stage yet, who have an important function as perverted doubles of parental figures: a seducer-judge, a dead father who was a general, a prostitute, an invasive aunt.

This small world inevitably spins like a merry-go-round on one pivot, the phallic question, a question so conflict-laden for the heroine Hedda, who has substituted this phallus with a deadly object whose role in the play is essential: her father's revolver.

Lovborg, the main male character, a brilliant intellectual, is an alcoholic. This alcoholism started at the time of his chaste yet stormy love relationship, in the past, with Hedda. The day he tried to take advantage of her, she fired the famous revolver at him— and missed. After that he sank into drink and left the city.

Hedda marries a dull-witted academic, Tesman, who boasts a laughable erudition. He must soon publish a book.

The play opens with Hedda and Tesman returning from a long honeymoon trip. Suddenly, under the guise of business-as-usual, the fundamental questions are posed, which we might sum up as: What is a father? What is a woman and her desire?

Tesman shows his total obtuseness toward these questions. The book he is writing is as ridiculous as the prospect of his fatherhood, as we can infer when his Aunt Julie asks him about the dwelling she's found for them:

Miss Tesman: And what do you think of it all?

Tesman: I'm delighted! Quite delighted! Only I can't think what we are to do with the two empty rooms between this inner parlour and Hedda's bedroom.

Miss Tesman: [Laughing.] Oh my dear George, I daresay you may find some use for them—in the course of time.

Tesman: Why of course you are quite right, Aunt Julia! You mean as my library increases—eh?

Tesman's doltishness becomes all the more disturbing as we soon learn that his wife is already pregnant.

The Alcoholic

The equivocation and equivalence *book* ~ *child* are immediately put on the table.

The drama comes to a head with the return of Lovborg, accompanied by a flattering rumor: he has in fact just written a book that everyone's desperate to see. Besides that, Lovborg *has recovered from his alcoholism*. (Isn't this a clear proof that the Consul's hope had psychological truth?)

Yet Ibsen provides us with considerably more than this fragmentary element. He goes to the very roots of the problem. What miracle could have prompted this metamorphose? It can only be a woman, and a well-named one at that: *Thea*. God always intervenes in the life of men by way of the feminine, as one of Lacan's last sayings points out.

Thea appears on stage before Lovborg, entirely unaware of his past relations with Hedda. Between these two rivals from way back—they knew each other in their girlhoods—an apparently innocuous dialogue begins, in which Hedda, however, makes an outrageous slip of the tongue:

Hedda: And I shall say *du* to you and and call you my dear Thora.

Mrs. Elvsted: My name is Thea.

Hedda: Why, of course! I meant Thea...

What strange intention—and what art!—made Ibsen put in this Thora, the Book itself, here?

Hedda wants to penetrate the secret of Lovborg's withdrawal:

Hedda: Tell me, Thea, how did it start, this ... friendship?

Mrs. Elvsted: Oh, little by little... It's as if I had a sort ... yes, a sort of power over him...

Hedda: I see, and you, little Thea, you made a new man of him!

[Thea, turning over the 'key' to the mechanism:]

Chapter 5

Mrs. Elvsted: He would talk to me a long time about books.... When he had finished a chapter of the book he was working on, he would dictate it to me.

To write a book for a woman you love, in this relation to God recalled by Thea, has, by a strange couvade, cured the alcoholic, allowing him to be a father, albeit in a still imaginary, still delicate way.
Lovborg's stage entry confirms this frailty, this latent paternal unworthiness.
Now all the characters are gathered together and the discussion revolves around Lovborg's successful book. To the compliments he receives, he responds with contempt toward his "progeny." He tosses it onto the floor, denies it. The book is of no importance to him, it's nothing but a sketch for the real work, the book of books, the manuscript he brandishes before them. It's written in the hand of Thea, to whom he's dictated it.
"My true book," he declares, "is written in a woman's hand. *I planted the seed, she produced it.*"
The equivalency *book* ~ *child* rebounds, takes on definition.
Jealous, Hedda secretly decides to wreck this splendid edifice; she doesn't believe in Lovborg's new-won sobriety, and prods him. As the good hysteric she is, she hatches a plot.
One may question her reasons. Certain expressions give us a glimpse into her fundamental phantasm: she is a priestess of those cruel ancient mother-religions of Bacchus, and dreams of a bacchanal in which the sacrificial victim would be Lovborg.

HEDDA: And what came of it all, in the end?

TESMAN: Well, to tell the truth, I think it might best be described as an orgie, Hedda.

HEDDA: Had he vine-leaves in his hair?

As opposed to Eve-Thea, she is also Lilith, Lucifer's wife, the abortionist, the infanticide.
She goads Lovborg on to a drinking binge in which, "crowned in vine leaves," he will declaim his text.

The psychic space seems cloven into two regions between which the hero oscillates, that of the Book and the father, and that of alcohol and the mother, each presided over by a priestess.

Lovborg from here on is in space II, where the Book has no place.

In fact, what Lovborg does with his book, which Tesman has described as "extraordinary, one of the most remarkable works that has ever been written," is, quite simply, to misplace it. Lovborg has denied the first book; the second, he has allowed to drop out of sight. But Tesman has gathered it up and turned it over to Hedda, who hides it.

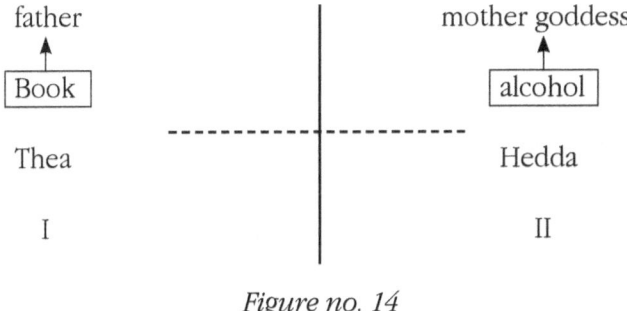

Figure no. 14

In her despair, Thea explains the symbolic web of the action:

Mrs. Elvsted: Do you know, Lovborg, that what you have done with the book—I shall think of it to my dying day as though you had killed a little child.

Lovborg: Yes, you are right. It is a sort of child-murder.

Hedda rises up against these "wild imaginings": "Well—but when all is said and done, you know—it was only a book—"

Yet shortly after, alone, she takes up the equivalence herself: she burns the manuscript, almost in a state of hallucination: "Now I am burning your child, Thea! —Burning it, curly-locks! The child Eilert Lovborg has given you. I am burning it—I am burning your child."

Beforehand, she pushes Lovborg to suicide, giving him one of her father's two revolvers. She advises him to aim for his heart. Yet Lovborg kills himself with a bullet to the lower abdomen, in a

Chapter 5

Real castration—he for whom that Symbolic had not been clearly inscribed.

But Hedda's intrigue aborts: Thea has a draft saved. With the help of Tesman, Hedda's husband, the book can be reconstructed. As for the pregnant Hedda, she falls into the clutches of the judge-seducer, whose attempt at blackmail she foils by shooting herself.

Thus Ibsen, thanks to this character of Hedda, provides us, in a remarkable round-trip voyage, with, on the one hand, a recovery from ethylism through the Book, a frail recovery, a reversible, prosthetic repair and, on the other hand, a relapse when the book vanishes.

Surer healing from this illness would no doubt require an earlier, complementary approach, where the subject would, as best he could, sort out the question of his own filiation.

CONCLUSION

Does returning to Freud and showing a fresh interest in his works imply a certain return to Judaism, to its great works? And why should this hypothesis be so unnerving, prompt such embarrassed silence among the scholarly clerics, rather than judgment based on actual evidence?

Will I be accused of wanting to re-Judaize psychoanalysis? The risk of that is slight, for reasons of structure. Judaism has shown, throughout history, in contrast to every other cultural system, a unique *centrifugal* proclivity, continually and discreetly inspiring, creating by detachment of its branches new doctrines, daughter religions, inventions. What cultural space has not profited by this incessant centrifuge, this dismemberment of a body that at every stage seems to exhaust itself in its new creature and yet, having lost blood in the process, starts off towards new discoveries?

And what return can be involved here for us, subjects who have forsworn any premise of Revelation?

This renunciation does not eliminate the vast treasure that, for a psychoanalyst at any rate, lies in the yellowed folios of these great texts: the logic of the signifier has been carried to its perfection, the relation of subject to object, posited as fundamentally lost, a deeply and relevantly, and the conditions and *a porias* of all practical thought, all ethics, magisterially defined.

We have contented ourselves, in this book, with looking into one single, especially thorny question: dietary rites.

A key to interpretation appeared as universal, applicable elsewhere to other rites, those that regulate space and time: every rite aims to create discontinuity out of a continuum, to apply the grid of the Symbolic, of language, onto the Imaginary of men and the Real of things.

The examination of dietary rites gives prominence to an unconscious and fundamental activity: the human being eats words, materialized in writing, organized into the Book.

Conclusion

In eating the Book, a depository of the murmuring desires of the earlier generations that determine us symbolically, the subject identifies himself with the group that has witnessed his birth, a group fundamentally structured by religion. At the same time the enigmatic advent of procreation takes place in that subject: the masculinity of the father, the feminity of desire.

Thus every human being not totally mad necessarily identifies with a group that provides him, through his language, the categories for thinking and building the framework of his phantasm. And there is this trivial and strange fact that conditions the others: individuals gather into communities, sharing a feeling of possessing who knows what common ether. In normal times the matter seems so natural that this basic relation goes unnoticed. But when the storm gathers, the bond takes on urgency, and seems to justify the risk of endangering one's life.

Why did it take until this century, and Freud in particular, to posit this question of the group and the play of identifications that structures it?

We must admit that the only issue at stake here is what goes wrong and creates a symptom. And without a doubt the relation of the individual to the group has becomes the most problematicof all. The intermixing of peoples, globalization of the economy and of cultures have profoundly shaken, even destructured human systems, tearing the social fabric apart down to its very framework. Our time, the only one we have and must live in, is meanwhile filled with unbreathable air.

Through its reflection on narcissism and the group, psychoanalysis, beyond its practice marked by intimacy, has from the beginning, entered into a dialogue with the whole of culture and urbanity.

The cause of these upheavals? Beyond episodic events and eternal ideological conflicts, their abrupt radicalization is attached to the irruption into human history of the discourse of science, its ever more assured hegemony over the economy, which explodes the best established cultural structures.

Here we can only hark back to a fundamental thesis of Lacan's: we are the subjects of science, and out of that fact comes a malaise of a new, extreme sort, the damaging effects of which psychoanalysis sets about to mop up.

A curious path! Born under the sign of Enlightenment, the outcome of scientific discourse contradicts the hopes of its pioneers. To the credo of universality its proffers opposed unprecedented phenomena of concentration and human segregation, linked to the mode of production and paving the way for totalitarianism. By what strange curse? That of the very act that institutes it.

The outcome of the scientific operation conducted on every man, and primarily over the learned, is a *desubjectivization*: science returns everyone, in depressive angst, to his final truth, that of a little bit of flesh, one scrap among others.

Faced with such a threat of annihilation, subjectivity revolts, convulsively; a subjective revolt alluring in aspect and yet in its blindness an agent of barbarity. A revolt often congealed at its point of birth, the individual, who has decided to manifest his existence and make a mark, for example, by choosing deviance. Yet the logic of the conflict extends further.

The group, despite the shackles it imposes, quickly appears as the best shield for the subjectivity of its members. So here it is recreated, exalted over its own ashes.

The profusion of movements, sects with motley ideologies and various chapels, falls within this tendency, bearing the odd suicidal fascination that all narcissistic exaltation entails. This frenzied quest for shaky "identities" has clearly underscored, with the clarity of caricature, the function of the Book in the structuring of groups. Every one of them has its manifesto, its canonical book: remember those sizable masses brandishing a little book, red in some parts of the world, green elsewhere? The conquest of power, its management, its crises, always encounters the strategic agency of the Book.

But the subjective revolt now enters into a third phase. For these exercises carried out to control groups and the Book, there is no better know-how than the old religions. Only yesterday they were thought to be quite dead, but a new vigor suddenly seems to be swelling their sails. Little by little, yet more and more quickly, the religions take back in hand—and what a firm hand it is!—that serious thing the secular powers have brought to an impasse: *jouissance*.

This unexpected return, in which barbarism makes out so well, signifies that the great clergies know better than anyone how to channel the torrents of wounded subjectivity.

Religion is never a matter of a momentary situation or of fashion. It emerges from the root of the human phenomenon. It has done so ever since there have been beings capable of speaking, and will

Conclusion

no doubt vanish only with the last such beings; it is the bone of the unconscious, the compromise that maintains the attachment to the mother in compliance with the Law, the brake put to fratricidal murder, the glowing ember smoldering beneath the ashes. It takes only the wind of hardship to make it a blazing flame.

The maniacal homogenization that science imposes is thus countered with subjective revolt, with the return of groups and of religions. On what turf? The only one that counts in these questions, the political one in which everyone is measured against the other in a search for the most favorable compromise to enter into a new millennium. Will the Book still have its function there?

Faced with the growing display of such forces, the place of the psychoanalyst seems quite ridiculous, precarious, yet also valuable and unique. To his human brother, congenitally ill with his humanity, the Freudian art offers a recourse against the misdeeds of a time that in broad daylight reveals the cornerstone of the edifice: madness.

APPENDIX

SIGNIFYING TRANSFERENCE[125]

Freudian studies, for all their diversity, generally proceed from the same line of thought. In an initial determination, we can call it conceptual. The term, "drive" for example, is privileged, then questioned in its sources, its meanings, its evolution in the thinking of Freud and of his students. We might therefore also call this method "synchronic," "vertical," or even "thematic."

Freud himself took this privileged path when he undertook the project of his *Metapsychology*, a project he nonetheless abandoned. Lacan also seems to prefer this path in his *Seminar XI: The Four Fundamental Concepts of Psychoanalysis*. The conceptual approach thus appeared as the most serious, indeed as the sought-after ideal.

No one would think to deny the necessary character of the method that responds to the elementary desire to understand. The spread of Freudian thought, moreover—unlike that of Lacan—essentially operates along this thematic track. Certainly, our remarks do not intend to challenge the conceptual approach, but merely recall the dangers, or in any case the limits, of the method, and also show—in the act—that it isn't unique, and at the same time question the instrument itself.

The conceptual method in effect involves dangers, those resulting from the privilege accorded to signification, to imagination, indeed to the "idolizing" of concepts. It tends, to a greater or lesser extent, to reabsorb the heterogeneity of the Freudian text, to return the singularity of analytic discourse to preexisting, essentially philosophical, universals. Above all it presents limits: experience quickly returns the

---

[125] The argument of this text was presented in a lecture at the *Université de Bruxelles – Institut Martin-Buber*, November 1981.

Appendix

insight one takes for granted to the discouraging feeling that the object, apparently grasped in the concept, has slipped away. Understanding quickly becomes an obstacle unto itself.

Yet doesn't the vogue for this method extend well beyond the analytic field to the point of lending its style to our cultural situation? Let's venture the hypothesis that the current debate of ideas, a thematic debate (religion, racism), seems preoccupied by a keen wish to unpack metaphors, all metaphors, an ideal presented as desacralization. Unbeknownst to itself, thought gets more and more taken up in this game, fascinated by, indeed stuck to the metaphors one has the illusion of getting past.

If this hypothesis is true, today's cultural situation might be characterized by the accent it places on metaphoric thought. Its impasse comes from that incurable itch to "metaphorize metaphor" in the vain hope of finally reaching a metalanguage that would free us from language itself.

To be sure, it is a matter here of extreme positions into which every conceptual approach doesn't necessarily fall, but it seems necessary to locate them at the root of an apparently "natural" procedure.

Freud perceived these limits and dangers, as evidenced by the project, aborted and never resumed, of the *Metapsychology*, reduced to three articles, far removed, moreover, from what one might term a "conceptual approach." Perhaps only Lacan, whose oeuvre is not unduly weighed down by a concern to trot out definitions, seems to have understood the tacit warning. Rather, he seeks to carve out another path for reading Freud, where the symbolic would prevail, where *significance* predominates over *signification*, where, finally, topology and mathemes would constitute stops to the drift of understandings.

At least a second methodological path exists, then, alongside the prevailing one: that of the mathemes. No one is unaware that the mathemes remain a project, a problematic project since the paths of their development remain to be blazed: Will we ever manage to go beyond Lacan's algebraic notations or do they belong strictly to his own teaching style? How are we to achieve the strategic alliance of psychoanalytic theory and logic?

I propose a detour, another path for reading Freud's writings, which might sound simple if not simplistic: rather than a vertical synchronic study of concepts, a "horizontal" approach, *a systematic chronological reading*—omitting no text, however minor—an approach that would aim less at digging for discoveries than questioning the very train, the progress, of the thought, the connections, the involuntary associations that the various texts themselves make. The method would take its cue from the golden rule of free association. Rather than visit the countries arrived at, we would be interested in the voyage itself, in the paths that Freud managed to take in order to say what he said. Which is to say: How did Freud frame his questions? Practically speaking, it is a matter of reading the *Standard Edition*—since its equivalent still doesn't exist in German, much less in French. The method, heavy as it may seem, is immediately fertile and at once provides certain valuable results. It allows us to recall, first of all, that the different Freudian concepts can only with difficulty be isolated from one another, that they indubitably form a Borromean chain. This method draws up a clear cartography of Freud's oeuvre with various high summits—in chronological order: the neurotic symptom; childhood amnesia; the signifying mechanisms of the dream, the lapsus, and the joke; the theory of drives, etc. But it's a cartography that also reveals shadows: What footbridges led Freud from one massif to the other? Today we easily conceive how the first link in the chain arose, the discovery of the unconscious in the hysterical symptom. Yet we don't immediately see, or see only quite approximately, what leads from Anna O. to the *Interpretation of Dreams*, and then to *Three Essays on Sexuality* or *Totem and Taboo*. So Freud did not find waiting for him on the couch some delicacy baked to perfection, wrapped up for him with a ribbon. Careful, thorough examination of his complete works thus shows the hiatuses, the deep gaps and fault-lines, whose very way of crossing and over-leaping raises a question.

To answer that question does not seem unfeasible, since a close reading reveals Freud's habit of marking these passages with small but immensely far-reaching texts. Let's consider one concrete example, among the most important. In his *Studies on Hysteria*, the symptom is resolved thanks to the coming to light of certain repressed memories—memories contemporary with the forming of the symptom. It isn't a question, then, of determinations by childhood and still less of childhood amnesia. The mechanism producing the symptom is hysterical amnesia.

Several years later, Freud will broach the question of childhood, of the amnesia that masks it, and underlines its importance. But, let

Appendix

me insist, the passage from hysterical amnesia to childhood amnesia is not a given. There's a gap there.

Freud would cross over this fault-line in 1899, in a famous and fundamental article on screen memories. How will he operate? By drawing a point-by-point parallel between the hysterical symptom and childhood life.

That the events lived through in earliest childhood are very important was not a startlingly new notion, even in the nineteenth century: educators had forever known this, and Freud begins by recalling this principle, in order to add to it immediately an essential remark. If these events have such force, how do we explain that they are generally forgotten and that memory takes on its structure only from six or eight years of age? The Freudian step is there, in the clear pointing out of this paradox—the same as the one he disclosed in hysterics.

Yet the next step is far more disturbing: Freud ventures the hypothesis, quickly transformed into a thesis, that the knowledge revealed in analysis of the hysterical symptom can be transposed, pretty much as it is, to the psychology of the child, apparently for the mere reason that in both cases the same term *amnesia* comes up in relation to important events.

How should we refer to this methodological leap? Surely it immediately suggests *analogy*, albeit a peculiar, quite audacious use of analogy en route to this putting in place of an essential piece of theory. We know the sort of epistemological contempt that a long philosophical tradition has for the use of analogy, especially pushed to this extreme. Does the term even suit this founding operation, or isn't our language suffering here from a signifying gap?

The pursuit of our "horizontal" reading reveals another major surprise: once we've sighted this mechanism of analogy, we'll find it, massive, essential, at all the fertile moments in the oeuvre.

On at least two occasions, the procedure is openly acknowledged. On the one hand, in "Obsessive Acts and Religious Practices," Freud, starting from the same word *ritual*, attempts to transpose established knowledge about obsessional neurosis into the religious domain. On the other hand, Freud extends this intuition in *Totem and Taboo*, where he pairs psychoanalysis and anthropology in a mutually illuminating exchange, and does so for the reason given in the first lines of the work: the source of the neuroses is to be found in *childhood*, and primitive peoples can be considered the *childhood* of humanity.

Signifying Transference

Once again, whether it be such disparate fields as psychoanalysis and anthropology, or within the field of psychoanalysis a consideration of questions that are *a priori* quite distinct, the existence of the same word irresistibly impels Freud to repeat his strange analogous operation, supported, yet also masked by clinical observation. The sharper the reader's perspicacity becomes, the more he steadily discovers that this operation recurs, subtler with each new step, omnipresent in the oeuvre, until it is finally revealed to be one of Freud's foundations, one of his fundamental intuitions.

Let's take a short inventory of this. The first works are no doubt the most instructive. The assured starting point: the deciphering of the hysterical symptom, which generally reveals "some stupid wordplay." From that point, Freud can confidently undertake the interpretation of dreams. Isn't it analogous to the symptom, a rebus, a pun that uses as privileged materials what's succumbed to amnesia? Always by analogy, the slips, then jokes, reveal their enigma. Freud therefore carries out a series of sensational slides of analogy (verified through his clinic), depending each time on scant resemblances, most often a simple word. The fecundity of the operation is amazing.

Later on, the religious question will be broached in the same way. The analogy with the biology of monocellular organisms will help to formulate *Beyond the Pleasure Principle*, and finally the parallel will be drawn between *Mass Psychology and the Analysis of the Ego*.

But here we have, at last, the main use of this singular method: *Übertragung*, transference. Freud communicates this essential discovery to us, this birth act of psychoanalysis, in the last pages of his *Studies on Hysteria*. The feelings, acts, words that the patient comes out with in treatment are the analogue of other, earlier, forgotten ones, linked to that primitive phase of exclusive attachment to the parental nucleus. Once again, then, a set of totally disjointed facts: the behavior presently displayed by the the patient vis-à-vis someone who is basically a stranger, the analyst, and that which the patient experienced under radically different circumstances, far removed in space and time. It takes some self-assurance, not to say nerve, to propose to deduce the signifiers of the one on the basis of the other, a nerve for which Freud gives us—and could he?—no reason. Later on, he will excuse himself: "...it is not possible to avoid applying certain abstract ideas to the material at hand, ideas derived from

Appendix

somewhere or other but certainly not from the new observations alone."[126]

The finest illustration of this procedure is probably to be found in the article "The Theme of the Three Caskets."[127] Freud uses two plays by Shakespeare, a comedy, *The Merchant of Venice*, and a tragedy, *King Lear*. The former contains the episode of the *three* caskets, the latter that of King Lear's *three* daughters. The occurrence of the term *three* is enough for Freud to identify their significations.

The "analogical" method thus seems to occupy the entire Freudian field, a unique situation in Western thought, no doubt one of the sources of the heterogeneity of psychoanalysis within the cultural panorama. If this discipline gets bad press there—despite being so well known—the systematized use of a methodology discredited, rejected, abhorred by all our philosophical *savoir-vivre* may perhaps play an important part. It is a curious fact, however, that no epistemologist seems to have pointed out this place of analogy in Freudian thought, nor any critic seized on the argument to raise an objection of principle to it, nor pointed out the enormity of the phenomenon, a universal blindness that, evidently, has all the characters of a symptom.

This blindness is not one Freud shared; he knew the function that analogy played in his way of thinking and, himself, raised the objection to it.

> A warning must be uttered at this point. The similarity between taboo and obsessive sickness may be no more than a matter of externals; it may apply only to *forms* in which they are manifested and not extend to their essential character. Nature delights in making use of the same forms in the most various biological connections: as it does, for instance, in the appearance of branch-like structures both in coral and in certain chemical precipitates. It would obviously be hasty and unprofitable to infer the existence of any internal relationship from such points of agreement as they, which merely derive from the operation of the same mechanical causes. We shall bear this warning in mind, but we need not be deterred by it from proceeding with our comparison.[128]

---

[126] S. Freud, "Instincts [sic: i.e. Drives] and Their Vicissitudes" (1915), in *S.E.*, vol. XIV, 117.

[127] S. Freud, "The Theme of the Three Caskets" (1913), in *S.E.*, vol. XII, 291-301.

[128] S. Freud, *Totem and Taboo*, in *S.E.*, vol. XIII, 26.

Freud was not unaware of the objection, but with the same splendid assurance, here as on each occasion that he drew on this analogy, he decided to press on, without hesitation or ... justification.

Before going further, however, it becomes necessary to sort out a point of vocabulary. The term "analogy" evidently doesn't seem to take account of the operation in play. It isn't a matter of just suggestively drawing a parallel, but rather of active transport from one domain to another. Since our vocabulary does not seem to possess an adequate term for this figure of the logic of the signifier, I propose to coin a term, *signifying transference* [*la transférance signifiante*], to account for the main mechanism of analysis.

What justified Freud in this operation so contrary to our ways of demonstration? No doubt the firm support of his clinic. But didn't he himself tirelessly repeat that the clinic only takes shape out of the questioning brought to it, which comes "certainly not from current experience alone"?

The main justification would be as follows: Freud always confined the use of signifying transference, despite the initial remoteness from the nearer domains, to a single domain, that of human phenomena, the phenomena-effects of the structure of language. A few rare side-steppings of this field, such as the comparison made in passing to the biological sphere in *Beyond the Pleasure Principle*, remain incidental. Despite suggesting as much, Freud never transposed the data of the mineral world to psychic reality. The recourse to analogy in the study of human facts becomes defensible if they are effects of a single structure; and, when those effects are identical (amnesia, ritual, etc.), why not infer, for the span of a hypothesis, that they were engendered by the same elements of this structure and are to be deciphered by the most open route? At this point, we may ask: Is it even a matter of analogy?

Another question: From where did this bent, this passion, come to Freud, and from where did his incomparable virtuosity in handling signifying transference come?

Let me say, without beating about the bush: it came from the umbilicus of his thought, which binds him to his culture of origin, Judaism—and Judaism, at that, in its least-known aspect. Signifying transference, isolated here with some difficulty, in fact exists there as one of the fundamental, common operations of the *Midrash*, the *gezera chava* ("same rules"). Take two Biblical verses, v1 and v2, situated at any point in the text, for instance, the first in Genesis, the second in Isaiah. The two verses contain the *same word* and we possess certain knowledge about this word in v1. The *gezera chava* allows us to transfer this knowledge of v1 to v2, without concern for context or plausibility. All that counts are the observed connections in the writing. We find this operation in Freud once again in regard to "amnesia," "ritual," "child"... an unprecedented operation! yet so illustrative of the startling train of thought of ancient *Midrash*. The procedure, incidentally, frightened off the rabbinical authorities pretty quickly in the high Middle Ages; they issued decrees banning any new *gezera chava* not considered in the Talmud. Unaware of the fact, Freud, then, was lifting an age-old ban on this figure of logic and, at the same time, considerably widening its application.

We can go further, verifying how illuminating the parallel between Judaism and psychoanalysis proves to be—and mutually so. Some essential, yet left in the shadows, corners of Judaism come into startling relief thanks to the Freudo-Lacanian experience; conversely, a practice of *Midrash* makes it easier to understand the signifying mechanisms at play in analysis.

The specialists of *Midrash* in fact considered the *gezera chava* as the generalization of another more fundamental interpretative operation, the *semukha*: two juxtaposed verses, however heterogeneous their apparent meaning, possess, beyond this, a logical link, and may be read as a single utterance. To take an example: "Miriam died. The well was drained." The *semukha* leads us to deduce that the supplying of water for the wells came from Miriam's merits. So it privileges the contiguities, the connections of the text, thus giving the Talmud its style.

Let us recall that certain rabbis considered this rule to be the fundamental principle of Judaism, indeed—however paradoxical and forgotten it may seem—the criterion of the Jew that he always carries about with him, as it were on the soles of his shoes. There is no need to keep repeating that Freud used this principle again until, with the *Traumdeutung*, it became one of the best points of reference for the day-to-day work of the analyst.

The *gezera chava* thus generalizes the *semukha*, the latter requiring literal contiguity, by artificial creation of continuity as soon as two utterances contain the same word. "One draws out"— the Tamudic expression used here—one extracts the verses from the dross of a given context to juxtapose them and carry out the transference.

Let us come back to Freud and state that the principle of interpretation according to which "two contiguous statements *a* and *b* must be read *ab*," in other words the *semukha*, itself merely extends, one of the two fundamental mechanisms of the primary process of the unconscious, *Verschiebung*, or displacement.[129]

Displacement, we know, plays a decisive role in our psyche. "It is the means by which the unconscious most aptly eludes censorship."[130]

If we admit the fundamental thesis that the unconscious is the trace, the alluvium deposited in us by language, displacement is conceived as the effect of a well-known rhetorical figure, which consists of designating the totality of a thing by its part, or by what is contiguous to it: metonymy.

What does this detour, this interweaving of psychoanalysis and the Talmud teach us?

First of all, a heightened perception of the startling coherence of Freud's body of work: the signifying transference proceeds from generalization to the whole of the analytical theory of mechanisms of contiguity and displacement—in the same way that the *gezera chava* generalizes the *semukha*. We have been able to state this proposition thanks only to the recommended "horizontal" method—henceforth qualifiable as metonymic—and such an idea could only have come to us because we have been introduced to the reading of the Talmud. In this light, Freud's entire oeuvre appears to be one huge metonymy; and psychoanalysts are well advised to let themselves be swept away, at least once, by the wave of this text.

There is also this: the *gezera chava* offers the advantage of being able to be stated in mathematical terms, precisely in the language of sets. We must therefore attempt the following:

Let there be two subsets, belonging to the set *A* of language, structured by a certain number of logical operations. If these two sub-

---

[129] The sign that Freud well understood displacement and transfer in this dimension of signifying transference is clearly shown in this passage in *Totem and Taboo* (*S.E.*, vol. XIII, p. 27): "I would like at present to put side by side two examples of the transference [or as it would better be termed, the *displacement*] of a prohibition."

[130] J. Lacan, "L'instance de la lettre"/ "The Instance of the Letter in the Unconscious," in *Écrits*, (Paris: Éditions du Seuil, 1966) *Écrits*, translated by Bruce Fink (New York: W.W. Norton, 2006).

sets present *one* common property, we can posit that at least one operation is also common to both.

Example: childhood memories and those of the hysteric as sets having a common property we are familiar with: amnesia. What structuring operation recognized for hysteria also obtains for childhood? Sexual experiences.

Such would be the definition of the Freudian signifying transference.

Up to this point, the greatest benefit has come from the illumination brought by Judaism to psychoanalysis, but the reverse is true as well.

Here we are able, for instance, to respond to a question I posed elsewhere, with reference to the Talmud. What is essential in the Talmud text is in effect presented as unreadable to an "outside" reader who does not fully enter into the game. The reason comes from the systematically ridiculous character of the issues taken into consideration and concerned with the most humdrum daily life, from the building of huts to menstruation. What does this ridiculousness signify that was such a mystery for us? A realism pushed to its furthest limits, in raw form, beside which minute Balzacian descriptions seem flamboyant metaphors. The singularity of the Talmud lies in its systematic exercise of metonymy.

If we remember Lacan's teaching that metonymy "operates from a metabolism of *jouissance*," then Talmudic style does not sink to the level of a simple academic formalism but becomes homogeneous with its project to constitute a desiring textual machine, providing the subject inscribed in it, the Jew, with a sort of instruction manual for an unsinkable *jouissance*.[131]

The essential thing about the Talmud is this extreme realism. But it's not its totality. The rest of it is composed of small narratives, *machal*, far more developed in the Midrashic literature. The *machal* is comparable to allegory.

This isn't the place to open up the question, so essential to literature, above all medieval literature, of the status of allegory. Does it come mainly from metaphor or metonymy? How is the one connected

---

[131] J. Lacan, *Radiophonie*, *Scilicet* nos. 2 & 3 (Paris: Éditions du Seuil, 1970) [also in *Autres écrits*. Éditions du seuil, 2001, 403-447 –trans.]

Signifying Transference

to the other? It is clear that the *machal* chiefly seeks an effect of signifying transference; in the Talmud it remains on the track of metonymy.

Delving into these questions would be of utmost interest to penetrate further into Hebrew literature. This literature in fact may be subdivided into two large parts, which most of the great Jewish theologians have viewed as closely interconnected: the Talmud on the one hand, the Kabbalah on the other, text that differed radically in their style. The extreme realism of the one is opposed to the most vertiginous speculations of the other. Their very study proceeds differently: the thematic approach, if it is absurd for grasping the real spice of the Talmud, works well for the Kabbalah. The dominance of metonymy in the one is opposed to the triumph of metaphor in the other. Now, allegory is the privileged literary form of the Kabbalah, especially of the Zohar. Is it the tipping point at which metonymy is tied to metaphor?

ACKNOWLEDGMENTS

This book is the product of my singular and daily dialogue, throughout the 1970s, with Jacques Lacan.

A particular debt also binds me to my students at Paris VIII who, one Wednesday after another in the years 1981-83, followed, criticized, above all enriched with original work, my elaborations. The same recognition should go to those who entrusted me with the responsibility for their analysis. Some of them, without knowing it— though they will surely recognize themselves—made important contributions to this book. These debts fully confirmed the truth of the Talmudic adage: one learns more from one's pupils than from one's teachers.

Printing this book also allows me to repair an oversight. The first draft of this text allowed me to obtain the diplomas needed for my title of psychiatrist. Professor J.M. Alby, whom I thank, was quite graciously willing to take on the academic guidance of my labors and to encourage them.

My gratitude also goes out to Jean Guir, who played a valuable role in the publication of this book.

NEW AFTERWORD

TABLE, SIGNIFIER, AND IMAGE

The thesis developed in this book, of man as bibliophage, or an eater of writing, emerged as if from an epiphany after a long confrontation with certain theoretical impasses left by Freud. No, the construction in his *Totem and Taboo* definitely did not hold water, and its ruin left behind it a psychoanalytic edifice whose roof has been leaking heavily ever since. It was urgent to attempt its repair, a Talmudic *tikkun*.

Lacan used to speak of wanting to pick up matters where Freud left off. Why not dare to pick up matters where Lacan left them, and, since the grain of wheat has died, "let it bear much fruit"?

In place of the big aboriginal Darwinian ape, this primitive father of the horde murdered and devoured by his sons, I've substituted the Book as a Father also destroyed and devoured, as human history attests from its origins to our own days.

Twenty years have passed since the writing of these pages, which justify this brief rereading.

Those years saw the triumph of the structuralism of Lévi-Strauss and of Lacan, who repossessed the primacy of the symbolic, of language, the skeleton and nervous system of our psychic reality, and I regret that that time is no more. Psychoanalysis having, after various extravagances, abandoned this questioning, it has emerged as lacking inspiration, reduced to a matter of opinion about how the world's faring, which, clearly, is not at all happy.

To be sure, new justifications for my thesis, and highly unexpected ones at that, came up. I would merely cite that Egyptian statuette, seen in a showcase of the Archaeological Museum of Naples, whose body is entirely covered in hieroglyphic writings. It represents a healing god. The magician-therapist pours water over the head of the idol, water that slowly streams over his body. The liquid collected at the foot of the statue is administered to the sick person. The "water's memory," which made the news some years ago, was supposed to have captured the memory of the letters that the water had just dampened. Meanwhile, isn't this "memory of water" the same that the Muslim marabout relies on when he soaks in water a leaf covered with Koranic scripture? The letters apparently erased by the operation are assumed to be transferred into the liquid matter and are swallowed by the mentally ill person who has sought help.

We needn't come back to the case of peoples without writing or to the support I've found in Claude Lévi-Strauss's *Mythologiques*, showing the structural similarity between the founding myths of a group and their table manners. That the kitchen should be the privileged place for these myths implies that the text of these myths is "imprinted" in what one eats.

The examples of the Egyptian statuette and of peoples without writing show us that the phenomenon of absorption of writing—or its equivalent—is not the exclusive property of the monotheistic cultures, above all Semitic ones, but is universal. It is what constitutes a human being.

All that was certainly said and abundantly developed in the body of this book. If I am adding these few pages, it is obviously to say something else, to pierce the limits of my thesis and try to go beyond them. The neophyte's enthusiasm I drew from discovering the power of the symbolic, my impression, at that time, that it alone was worthy of interest, created those limits.

Symbolic structure forms the skeleton and the nervous system of our psychic reality, yet those forms can't subsist on their own. A body is required to bear them, and the flesh of this body is our imaginary. My refusal to consider this essential dimension led me at the time to evade a certain number of objections people could have raised.

The first of these objections, and a sly one at that, concerns Christianity. Through the sacrament of the Eucharist, the Christian faith would seem to enter perfectly into my scheme. Doesn't the worshipper, in taking communion, ingest the body of Christ, and doesn't that body, in being the Word incarnate, have the status of writing?

Yet how can we not see the fundamental difference between the liquid in which a *real* writing has soaked and the small wafer disk that is the host, which remains uninscribed by any concrete signifier, either directly or by some precise ritual structure? The faithful celebrant who swallows it is content to *imagine* ingesting the Word. There is a disconnection between the letter, the thought of preserving the spirit, and its ingestion. The real consumption of the letter is replaced by an imaginary ingestion. Christianity introduced, perhaps for the first time in human history, this disconnection between the letter, the Book, and table manners. For the Christian, all that is edible may be eaten without further ado, as he desires.

This new dispensation, which seems self-evident, in fact rests on a key text of the New Testament, of which full measure has yet to be taken, and which is designated as "Peter's Vision."[132]

> *In a trance I saw a vision. A certain vessel descended, as it had been a great sheet, let down from heaven by four corners; and it came even to me:/ Upon the which when I had fastened mine eyes, I considered, and saw four-footed beasts of the earth, and wild beasts, and creeping things, and fowls of the air./ And I heard a voice saying unto me, Arise, Peter; slay and eat./ But I said, Not so, Lord: for nothing common or unclean hath at any time entered into my mouth./ But the voice answered me again from heaven, What God hath cleansed,* that *call not thou common.*

Through this vision, Peter abolished all the Jewish dietary rules structured like a Book. If I can eat according to my whims, with no other rules or limits than those of my tastes, then the link between the act of eating and the signifier is abolished. The symbolic and food are hereby disconnected.

This text constitutes the true schismatic act between Judaism and earliest Christianity, in the same manner as do the teachings of Paul. Judaism never condemns general opinions. On the other hand, the theorized transgression of the code of rules, the *halacha*, does entail excommunication.

Pressing further this logic of the refusal to really eat the Book, the Church will place the reading of the Bible, the Book that founds it, on the index. This reading will be taken up again only with the explosion of the Reformation. Nonetheless, as one has to eat the Book, this book will now be *imaginarized* by way of the Eucharist.

---

[132] Acts of the Apostles, 11:1-9

New Afterword

Thus it is not just words that are eaten, but also *images*, and this is also true of Jewish and Muslim dietary rites.[133] It is the balance between Imaginary [I] and Symbolic [S] that varies and that Christianity overturns: primacy of S over I in Judaism, without the latter being absent; primacy of I over S in Christianity, without the Symbolic—the whole rite of the mass exists for this purpose— being abolished.

This veritable revolution in diet introduced by Christianity announces the eating *habitus* of modern man.

It is, indeed, the second objection that would have had to be raised, if psychoanalytic societies functioned like theoretical discussion forums: Does modern man, the subject of science, still eat the Book, and if so, which? Having rejected in its entirety his belief in Revelation, his reference to the Book has grown very pale, often nonexistent, but also with violent rekindlings. What, then, does the law of the universality of the ingestion of writing become? Taking stock of the imaginary dimension allows us to respond to this major objection.

Even a quick examination of our forms of nourishment allows for the following analysis: What do we eat today? *Food from the four corners of the globe*: Japanese sushi alongside Berber couscous, Neapolitan pizza alongside Indian curry. We go "ethnic," we eat "exotic," that is to say that we incorporate the *images* conveyed by these foods that have come from some country where we have spent, or would like to spend, vacation time, dream time, freed from the slavery of our daily grind. Amid jeans and colas, with a hamburger, we similarly consume the "American dream," which is always on the verge of becoming our current nightmare.

Are we, then, by this point, solely devourers of images, with no relation to any Book? By no means. Already those distant lands whose gastronomy we adopt have begu to influence our culture, our language, our practices. Hasn't the influence of yoga, of acupuncture, and

---

[133] An illustration recently found of this practice: in 787, at the second Council, the Fathers of the Council, to justify the sacred representations, gave "the example of a woman who, to recover from her pains, had absorbed fragments of a fresco of saints Cosmas and Damian, the healing saints, which she had had painted on the walls of her house: "... She straightened up, scratched a little bit from the plaster coating, tossed this scraping into water and drank down the mixture. All at once she was cured": in Philippe-Alain Michaud, "Adorer les surfaces," [Worshipping Surfaces], in "Images et religions du Livre," *Art Press*, no. 25, 2004.

of meditation received close support from Asian cuisine? Concern for medical dietetics, for calories, vitamins, cholesterol, trace elements, for "healthy eating," now, with reinforcement from ad campaigns, besets our relation to food.

Yet the essential question lies elsewhere. The disappearance of our obligatory reference to the revealed Books has not simply left behind it a scorched earth. Another book, no less commanding, the Book of science that governs our world—this is the Book we eat off our plates.

This Book of science that we now eat, with its Symbols and its Imaginary, is the most universal that humanity has ever known. In great strides it is bringing uniformity to the entire planet's diet. While a Parisian is eating sushi, a Japanese is eating hamburgers or pizza.

Perhaps we should consider certain movements against fast food and junk food as the legitimately nostalgic reaction to the loss of signifiers and images that structured our food: the Book of science, making its way even onto our plate, has deeply debilitated our relation to the Symbolic as well as our relation to our imaginative faculties.

Gérard Haddad
January 2005

Printed in November 2013
by Modulgrafica Forlivese (FC)

www.ingramcontent.com/pod-product-compliance
Lightning Source LLC
LaVergne TN
LVHW040144080526
838202LV00042B/3015